HOMOSEXUALITY:

A SCRIPTURAL WAY FORWARD FOR THE UNITED METHODIST CHURCH

JOE MILLER, JR.

EnerPower Press
Gonzalez, FL
2015

Cover Image: Dreamstime ID 19557560, © Nikkytok | Dreamstime.com - Beam Of Light Photo

Cover Design: Henry E. Neufeld

ISBN10: 1-63199-221-X
ISBN13: 978-1-63199-221-6
Library of Congress Control Number: 2015955968

EnerPower Press
P. O. Box 841
Gonzalez, FL 32560

enerpowerpress.com
pubs@energion.co
850-525-3916

This book is dedicated to all of my committed colleagues at Breaking the Silence in the Texas Annual Conference of the United Methodist Church. "Breaking the Silence (BTS) is a group of clergy and laity in the Texas Annual Conference of The United Methodist Church. We aspire to be a healing voice within the climate of fear and misinformation surrounding sexual orientation and gender identity."

Information on BTS at http://www.btsumc.org/.
All proceeds from this book will go to BTS.

TABLE OF CONTENTS

Part 2: The Possibility of Scriptural Unity within the United Methodist Church

INTRODUCTION

Homosexuality is one the most polarizing and confusing issues within the American culture, political arena, media, and church. Our culture has divided itself by acceptance and/or rejection of the LGBT community and/or gay sexual relationships. There seems to be little middle ground. Christians particularly are divided on various issues regarding the LGBT community. Is homosexuality (orientation and/or practice) a sin? Should homosexuals have equal rights to marriage, legal access, church leadership, inheritance, benefits, and clergy ordination? The government is obviously polarized and confused as evidenced by the Clinton administration's implementation of "don't ask, don't tell" in the military and its withdrawal in the Obama administration. The defense of marriage act (DOMA) was a political/societal attempt to preclude gay marriage by defining heterosexual marriage as the only acceptable norm.

The cultural tide towards acceptance and full inclusion of LGBT rights and privileges will eventually carry the day. Courts have overturned and continue to overturn state laws that preclude gay marriage. The Supreme Court recently ruled, 5-4, that the Constitution guarantees a right to same-sex marriage in the United States, but that does not answer the questions for the Christian church. What should Christians believe about homosexual relationships including marriage? Should we condone and participate in gay marriages?

Scientific and medical studies affirm that homosexuality is an orientation born of discovery rather than a lifestyle choice. In other words, homosexuality is a function of genetics and/or environment that causes a person to be attracted to the same sex rather than the opposite sex. There are arguments pro and con to what causes sexual attraction, but orientation is not chosen. There are some cases of homoeroticism, such as prison sexual contacts, that are not between homosexuals. The questions that this book attempts to address are the following: given that homosexual orientation exits in our world today, is it morally permissible (according to scripture) for those with said orientation to participate in homosexual eroticism and under what circumstances?

Younger generations of Americans are more accepting of LGBT inclusion, and they express dismay at what they perceive as hypocrisy in the church's homophobia. Within in the next 20 years we, as a society, will wonder why we ever excluded the LGBT community from full rights and privileges.

So, if the issue is becoming *fait accompli*, why do we need another book on homosexuality? Although society is moving toward full inclusion, the church is in the midst of great struggle that is cleaving the union of the one body of Christ. Some denominations have already experienced schism as a result of acceptance of gay marriage/union and ordination of gay clergy. Some years ago, the Episcopal Church ordained an openly gay bishop, Gene Robinson, and a number of American Episcopal churches severed their relationships with the Episcopal Church and covenanted with churches in Africa that were part of the Anglican Communion. The Presbyterian Church (USA) recently decided that pastors could officiate at same sex weddings in states where they were legal. The United Church of Christ has allowed gay marriage since 2005. The Evangelical Lutheran Church in America (ELCA) endorsed homosexual partners in 2009, homosexual marriage in 2011, and elected the first gay bishop in 2011. The Southern Baptist Convention and the General Conference of the United Methodist Church officially oppose gay marriage and the ordination of openly gay clergy. The Roman Catholic Church opposes gay marriage and their clergy are celibate, so it is a moot argument for priestly ordination.

The United Methodist Discipline (the official polity and doctrine of the UMC) officially opposes homosexual relationships. The requirements for ordination as clergy specify the following: "The practice of homosexuality is incompatible with Christian teaching.

Therefore self-avowed practicing homosexuals are not to be certified as candidates, ordained as ministers, or appointed to serve in The United Methodist Church."[1] The term "the practice of homosexuality is incompatible with Christian teaching" will be referred to as the "noninclusion clause" of the UMC in this book. It was added to the Discipline of the UMC in 1972. The UMC official stance on gay marriage is that "Ceremonies that celebrate homosexual unions shall not be conducted by our ministers and shall not be conducted in our churches."[2] In the same book of Discipline, there are words of grace extended to the gay community; regardless, the UMC recognizes gay sex as sinful. At the 2014 Annual Conference meeting of the Texas Annual Conference, a set of resolutions was put before delegates that would petition the General Conference to change discriminatory language in the Discipline. They were rejected by a margin greater than 2 to 1. Unofficial organizations within the UMC are at odds with one another over this issue: Breaking the Silence favors full inclusion and the Confessing Movement, supported by the periodical *The Good News*, supports the continued noninclusion clause. While this book may be of interest to all Christians, I am a United Methodist clergyperson and I write from my perspective and concern for my church. I hope to provide a way forward for the United Methodist Church to resolve the issue and put it behind us.

Some UMC pastors have violated this doctrinal admonition and performed gay marriages. The Rev. Frank Schaefer was defrocked on December 19, 2013, by the United Methodist Church for performing a gay marriage in Pennsylvania between his son and son's spouse. After much judicial proceedings, Schaefer was reinstated after serving a 30-day suspension. Retired Bishop Melvin Talbert performed a gay marriage in Alabama (actually a *blessing* because the couple was already married in Washington DC). The bishop was formally asked by the executive committee of the Council of Bishops of the UMC not to do the wedding, and the Council

---

1   *The UMC Discipline*, 304.3.
2   *The UMC Discipline*, 341.6.

of Bishops has formally written and asked him to submit himself
on charges to the Judicatory of the UMC. Many clergy have supported him and many clergy have called for his defrocking. There
have been unofficial dialogues suggesting that the UMC split into
two denominations and others are crying for unity between the two
groups. Of course many of the seven million members are caught
in the battle unknowingly. These are merely examples of what is
going on in my denomination.

Since homosexuality is such a polarizing subject for Christians,
what stance should the church take in providing spiritual direction
for Christians and to culture? Does it matter what the church does
or believes? Many in the church are oblivious to the issue or consider it a peripheral, unimportant argument among academics and
administrators. In his watershed book *Christ and Culture*, H. Richard Niebuhr proposes five typologies that define the relationship
of the church to its surrounding culture. If one adopts a typology
of the church as in relationship to culture in some way, what we
believe and what we do should matter greatly within the total cultural environment. If we become isolationists from culture, then
what we believe and do only matters to a church "behind the walls"
while culture goes about its secular business without our influence.
How we go about relating to culture is a massively complex issue.
This book takes the position that what we believe and what we
do are important to our culture and civilization. Ushering in the
Kingdom of God is more than bringing people into the Sunday
morning worship service; it is also impacting culture in a positive
way. The United Methodist Church's mission statement declares
that "The mission of the Church is to make disciples of Jesus Christ
for the transformation of the world. Local churches provide the
most significant arena through which disciple-making occurs."[3]
That phrase carries a lot of content to be unpacked, but one thing it
means is that the UMC is responsible, to some extent, for the moral
and spiritual character of the world around us. What we believe,
say, and do should make a difference in the societies of the world.

---

3   *The UMC Discipline* 120.

It matters what the church believes about homosexuality.

WHERE ARE WE TODAY?

Many churchgoers (if not most) today, both laity and clergy, are noninclusionists or "traditionalists" by belief. I define traditionalists as those who, if pressed to answer, would say that homosexuality is a sin. They might define the difference between orientation and homoeroticism. That is, they might say something like "hate the sin but love the sinner." If asked why they think homosexuality is a sin, they would refer generically to God's law, scripture, church teaching, and/or doctrine in a mostly obscure way. Some people would cite scripture out of context, such as "the Bible says it is an abomination." Whatever the specific response, I think most churchgoers would fall into this traditionalist group. Many who call themselves Christian but do not go to church would probably respond as traditionalist, as well. Of course, what the church believes and teaches should have nothing to do with individual opinion; our joint beliefs and teachings should be shaped by other, more transcendent sources and warrants. However, we cannot ignore what impacts the mindsets of individuals in the church because individuals impact the mindset of the church. Although expressed rather graphically, the traditionalist mindset equates with the opinion of Phil Robertson of *Duck Dynasty*, who made the following remarks in an interview in the January issue of GQ magazine: "It seems like, to me, a vagina — as a man — would be more desirable than a man's anus. That's just me. I'm just thinking: There's more there! She's got more to offer. I mean, come on, dudes! You know what I'm saying? But hey, sin: It's not logical, my man. It's just not logical."

Phil Robertson expresses what a lot of uneducated heterosexuals think. By uneducated, I mean those who still think that homoerotic behavior is a lifestyle choice made by people who are basically heterosexual. In other words, the belief exists that we are all heterosexual by creation, and some of us choose the homosexual lifestyle. This book does not debate the issue of choice versus orientation, because the issue does not exist. Homosexuality is a discovery or realization. There is no defense of flat-earth theory contained within this writing.

Another difficulty in discussing homosexuality is that open, honest, and real discussions about the details of homosexuality are difficult. One of the reasons for this lack of negotiability is the passionate polarization already mentioned. Another reason is our culture's reluctance to discuss sexuality and expressions of sexuality at all. As Archie Bunker (in the old TV classic that broke a lot of taboos) once said to Edith, "Paragorically.... I will not let you ever talk about our sex life." As long as gays stayed in the closet, traditionalists did not really have to be involved; they could just hope the issue would go away. There are some similarities to the civil rights movement in the 60s. African-Americans could not possibly stay in the closet, but if they would just stay in their place, some said, the whole issue would go away. Civil rights for people of color did not go away, and civil (and religious) rights for the LGBT community will not go away either.

Kids in my pre-sexual-revolution era may have joked about gay attributes, but it was like no such thing really existed. Today, that head-in-the-sand stance is gone. The issue is very much out in the open and being argued and tested. The LGBT community has been marginalized and oppressed for a number of years by both secular culture and religion. Much has been written in academic (psychological, sociological, theological) literature, the media has had a continuing field day, and our political/secular culture has relished the ongoing battle.

WHAT SHOULD THE CHURCH BE TEACHING?

We have noted the impact of tradition on belief, but tradition is a sticky wicket. Whose tradition? What timeframe in history? Recent tradition is clear in both the church and culture: traditionalists say that homoerotic behavior is anathema. But is the tradition consistent with experience, reason, and, most importantly, scripture itself? Traditionalists say that their tradition squares with scripture, and some quote various "clobber" scriptural texts that allegedly prove their point. These texts are bandied about and picked up piecemeal by the populace of pew sitters and church outsiders who both claim "values" as part of their agenda. This book is about those clobber texts and what they mean regarding homosexuality. Biblical interpretation is fraught with conflict, especially when it comes to a controversial subject.

Scriptures have been used to justify slavery, racism, ethnic prejudice, and elitism. The great theological arguments for and against slavery in the mid-1800s are an example. Plucked from context and interpreted literally, slavery was not only justified but proven as pre-ordained by God. The scriptures interpreted similarly have been and are being used to oppress and dominate women. The civil rights movement in this country was opposed by many well-intentioned (white) churches. There is a trajectory to the movement of the Holy Spirit among us, incorporating the living nature of holy scripture. Even the few years that separate the writing of the gospels show changes in the expectations of Jesus' return. It is quite natural and good that as the context changes over the years that the work of the Holy Spirit takes on new and exciting tasks. The gospel is truth, and the Holy Spirit represents the teachings and grace of Jesus Christ to us, but the application/context changes.

There are many books written about how to interpret biblical texts, but Adam Hamilton has written a book that is particularly helpful in understanding the Bible.[4] I do not intend to plow this ground that has been so ably cultivated by Hamilton, but I do want to emphasize two things. The first is context. Each book in the Bible was written within a particular context or set of contexts. The history that is covered and the history of the writing itself varies significantly. The creation stories in Genesis tell about something that happened in the distant past, but are told from the perspective of someone living much later. The oral tradition was passed down through the ages before being set in writing. The writing was also passed down through the ages while the language was changing, and various writers were redacting (editing) and adding various

---

4   Hamilton, *Making Sense of the Bible*.

other sources. Each writer or group of writers had their own agenda in repeating the story, and their readers were different in each generation. Occasionally, the readers or hearers were privy to details that make the biblical writing obvious to them but puzzling to us who came later. Those details were very much a function of the culture and scientific knowledge of the day. Of course, what is fascinating is that, through many hundreds of years, the Bible is relevant and revelatory as God's word to each generation. Paul's letters, such as Romans and 1 Corinthians were written to specific congregations or groups of congregations in the very early Church. Like today, each community of faith had its own set of issues that the apostle was trying to address through the written word. Scholars try to determine what was going on in those churches because we only have one side of the dialogue ... Paul's.

The other issue alongside of context is language. The First Testament was written in ancient Hebrew although it was translated into Greek in Alexandria Egypt about 200 BCE. This version is called the Septuagint, and many of the First Testament passages that Jesus and Paul use come from the Septuagint rather than the "original" Hebrew scriptures. Some First Testament quotations in the Second Testament vary from our own Bible because our First Testament is based on the Hebrew scriptures. Also, we do not have the "original" versions of any book in the Bible; we have what has been passed down to us. Scholars may spend their entire career interpreting old manuscripts and trying to develop the most "accurate" reading in the original languages. Even so, there are several versions of manuscripts, and that number increased with the discoveries of the Dead Sea Scrolls and the Nag Hammadi Library. From these manuscripts, interpreters have written numerous translations in English. There are more translations of the Bible into English than can easily be counted. There are several reasons for so many translations: we have recovered more ancient biblical manuscripts through the years, for one thing, and different translators try to balance readability with accuracy while pressing their own theological agendas.

Context and language are particularly important for interpreting the "clobber" texts that were referred to earlier. The context is very important because four clobber verses (1-4) in the Old Testament are part of narratives that are the genre of myth or epic, and they are very important theologically. The theology is missed by plucking the clobber versus out of context. Two others (5-6) are short texts that are part of a large series of commandments that were related in ways that are very different from our way of thinking. The interrelationship of these commandments makes them difficult to translate to our culture. The last three clobber verses come from Paul or the Pauline literature in the New Testament. In each of these letters Paul is addressing specific early Christian communities that each has a unique relationship with Paul. He is addressing that relationship and preaching to them about various issues in those specific churches. We cannot ignore the context of these letters.

Language is a difficulty in the majority of these verses for the simple reason that neither Hebrew nor Greek had a word for homosexual in their limited vocabularies. So these texts that have been used to declare homosexuality a sin have done so without the advantage of simple word translation. Specifically, in the Pauline scriptures that we will study, the translation and interpretation are very challenging, and various versions of the English Bible have vastly different translations of the clobber verses that appear in scriptures 7-9.

METHODOLOGY

Frank Schafer was driven by love to break the doctrinal standards of the United Methodist Church. He performed a marriage for his son because … well, he loves his son, and he did the ceremony out of love. There is some argument that focuses on comparing the biblical commandments with the overarching theme of biblical love. Some argue that God loves all of his creatures, including gay people; that Christ expresses the ultimate love and mercy of God for humankind; that we are commanded to love one another by

Jesus; and that God is love.[5] However, others would point out that sin is sin, and while forgiveness and mercy is always available through the death and resurrection of Christ, the need to obey the biblical commandments is not abrogated. Adultery is still adultery and murder is still murder, and our loving God is also just. However, what do the scriptures say? Since I am a Wesleyan by training and belief, I count scripture as the primary source for determining what the church's teaching and response should be on issues such as homosexuality. Reason, experience, and tradition—the remaining three legs of the Wesley Quadrilateral—also play a part in forming a sound framework for establishing moral positions. Hence the major portion of this writing is commentary on the nine clobber texts.

Other scripture exegetes have already plowed the ground of scripture and theology regarding homosexuality. Like many polarized questions, the answers are varied and also polarized. Although some authors are reasoned and objective, some seem to bring their own presuppositions to the subject, even when it comes to scriptural interpretation. Of course, exegetes are human and come to biblical interpretation with lenses impacted by culture, environment, ethnicity, experience, education, training, and personal and implanted paradigms. One of the overriding presuppositions is traditionally and culturally conditioned to find homosexual practice repugnant, distasteful, and very wrong. Hence, much of mainstream biblical commentary presupposes what is now assumed in our contemporary culture. On the other hand, those who have had and have intimate relationships with the LGBT community, either through pastoral relationships or secular relationships, tend to interpret the same scripture differently. Observing and pastoring LGBT individ-

---

5   John 3:16 *For God so loved the world that he gave his only Son, so that*
     everyone who believes in him may not perish but may have eternal life. John
     13:34 *"I give you a new commandment, that you love one another. Just as*
     I have loved you, you also should love one another. [35] *By this everyone will*
     know that you are my disciples, if you have love for one another." 1 Peter
     4:8 *Above all, maintain constant love for one another, for love covers a*
     multitude of sins. 1 John 4:8 *Whoever does not love does not know God, for*
     God is love.

uals and couples has become a motivation for many to favor the relaxing of doctrinal standards relating to homosexuality.

Traditional Bible commentaries support the noninclusion interpretation. The accepted exegesis of these verses declares homoeroticism as sinful behavior. Since a lot of voices have already established the prevailing belief, the prevailing understanding requires little study. Most of my efforts are focused on individuals who have employed a contrarian interpretation. Logically, one should have to prove (through scripture, reason, tradition, and experience) that something is sinful rather than prove it is *not* sinful. However, homoeroticism has been accepted as a sin by many, so more attention has to be paid to the opposite.

There are several sources available for our study: scripture is the primary source; presumably neutral commentary on the Bible (although my assumption is that most commentaries declare homoeroticism a sin); presumably neutral works on Bible-based ethics; specialized studies on the clobber scriptures that conclude that homoeroticism is either a sin or not a sin; and views expressed by different denominations.

There are new books on this subject coming out constantly. The various angles that they are coming from are fascinating. However, the biblical arguments are pretty much defined by now, and I have tried to cover the major foci of the argument. Hence, my analysis is very much dependent on selected scholars, and it is not comprehensive. I do not cover everything that has been said about this subject.

WHO IS DOING THE TEACHING TODAY?
ARGUING THAT HOMOSEXUALITY IS NOT A SIN

Jack Rogers is Professor of Theology Emeritus at San Francisco Theological Seminary, Moderator of the 213th General Assembly of the Presbyterian Church (USA), and author of the book *Jesus, the Bible and Homosexuality*. Although his experiences had to have had some effect on his stance, in the section of his book entitled

"How My Mind Changed,"[6] he credits his in-depth biblical study as the driving force for his efforts to effect change in the Presbyterian Church by giving equal status to the LGBT community. Of course, anyone who acts in a judicatory/administrative position within a major denomination and is making multiple decisions regarding the lives of congregations and preachers would have to be influenced by the relationships of the people and clergy. I find it fascinating that those clergy who deal with the gay community within their churches seem to be influenced positively and accept them as full Christians. The lens through which they read scripture may be different from those of us who do not minister to the LGBT community.

Adam Hamilton is pastor to the United Methodist Church of the Resurrection in Leawood, Kansas. It has become the largest United Methodist Church. Rev. Hamilton has also been swayed heavily by his ministry and relationships to the LGBT community in his own church. He is that rare individual who appreciates all of the counter arguments from other United Methodists but, over time, has taken a stronger and stronger position of his own. Chapter 29 in his most recent book, *Making Sense of the Bible*, expresses his scriptural interpretation of the biblical texts on homosexuality.[7]

J. Neil Alexander is a bishop in the Episcopal Church in Atlanta. Prior to becoming a bishop, he taught seminary and served parish ministry. In Chapter 3 of his short but important book, *This Far By Grace*, he details how he came to interpret scripture and how he now interprets it regarding homosexuality.[8] In the first two chapters of his book he details his encounters with a gay mentor and other LGBT people, but his focus is on biblical interpretation done "the Anglican way."

Daniel A. Helminiak published *What the Bible* Really *Says About Homosexuality* in 1994 that went through seven printings. A new and updated Millennium edition was published in 2000 and

---

6   Rogers, pp. 15-16.
7   Hamilton, *Making Sense*, Chapter 29, pp. 265-280.
8   Alexander, Chapter 3, pp. 21-50.

went through 12 printings. Helminiak is a Roman Catholic priest who has ministered to several gay communities. Like other clergy who have intimate relationships with the gay community, his biblical interpretations dispute the traditional, literal interpretations that have been used to oppress the LGBT community. His book is largely a scripture-by-scripture commentary that dismantles the interpretations that claim all homosexual practice is sinful.

John Boswell provided the initial in-depth, historical analysis of homosexuality and social intolerance in *Christianity, Social Tolerance, and Homosexuality*, published in 1980. In 1994, which is the year he died, his second book on gay marriage, *Same Sex Unions in Premodern Europe*, was published. Boswell was a professor of history at Yale University and an accomplished linguist; he was raised Episcopalian but converted to Roman Catholic at the age of 16. For his historic analysis he translated many ancient texts, poems, narratives, laws, philosophies, and the like, to try to understand the swinging pendulum of cultural practice and tolerance of homosexuality. He covered the chronological era from the beginning of the Western Christianity to the 14th century. Although attitudes swung by extremes over the centuries, in many historical eras, including early Christendom, the practice of homosexuality was not a religious, moral issue but a cultural issue. There was no recognition of gay orientation, and people of diverse backgrounds practiced both gay and straight sex. Many early rulers such as Emperor Hadrian had homosexual relationships. Boswell's analyses[9] of the scriptures and early church were an opening salvo against the contemporary, non-analytical acceptance of the status quo condemnation of the LGBT community. His scholarship is impeccable though, being the first to tackle this issue head on, his work has endured much criticism. Boswell died of AIDS at the age of 47, and I suspect that he was gay. Perhaps his personal experience informed his analysis.

The Rev. Dr. L. William Countryman is an Episcopal priest and, most recently, Sherman E. Johnson Professor in Biblical Stud-

---

9   Boswell, *Christianity*, pp. 91-168.

ies at the Church Divinity School of the Pacific, Berkeley, CA (now retired). He has written extensively on a number of theological, biblical, and Christian ethical subjects. Along with Boswell, Countryman took up the mantle of LGBT apologetics before it was popular to do so. His book *Dirt, Greed, & Sex*, published in 1988, was updated in 2007.[10] His work on homosexuality was motivated by a request for a series of lectures on the subject. He is responsible for pointing out the difference between "purity" and ethical or moral issues in the First Testament, particularly in Leviticus. He considers the purity issues more contextual to the time period and hence, less binding on contemporary society. Countryman is gay and married to Jon Vieira.

Mark Allan Powell is the Robert and Phyllis Leatherman Professor of New Testament at Trinity Lutheran Seminary. He is editor of the *HarperCollins Bible Dictionary* and author of more than 100 articles and 25 books on the Bible and religion, including a widely used textbook, *Introducing the New Testament*. He is probably the most prolific scholar within my selection of sources. Powell has written a chapter in a quasi-official book written by a series of distinguished authors in the Evangelical Lutheran Church of America (ELCA), *Faithful Conversations*, edited by James M. Childs.

In a somewhat surprising treatise by one of the leading Pauline scholars in the world, Victor Paul Furnish takes on the subject of homosexuality in the overall context of the moral teachings of Paul.[11] Furnish's view is surprising because he does not tell of any significant experience in relationships with gay persons; his entire book is about understanding the moral teachings of Paul. Furnish discusses divorce, sex, and marriage, and presents an entire chapter on homosexuality.[12] He points out the textual difficulties in making homosexuality practice a black and white issue. Dr. Furnish is University Distinguished Professor Emeritus of New Testament at Perkins School of Theology at Southern Methodist University.

---

10   Countryman, *Dirt, Greed, & Sex*.
11   Disclosure: Victor Paul Furnish was one of my professors in seminary.
12   Furnish, Chapter 3, pp. 55-93.

K. Renato Lings has recently published *Love Lost in Translation*, a 641 page tome made up of the most detailed literary and linguistic analysis of the clobber scriptures. Lings (according to book cover) and website holds degrees in Spanish, Translation Studies, and Theology. In addition to studying Latin, Greek, Hebrew, and Nahuatl (Aztec), he has written and taught extensively on biblical interpretation, translation, and issues relating to gender and sexuality. Missing from his introduction is his motivation for writing on this subject. His writing appears to betray only an academic interest in accurate translation and sexuality as expressed in the Bible. Although the book itself is very detailed in translation of Hebrew and Greek, it is a very readable and interesting book.

One of the more recent works is a very comprehensive, yet readable, book my Matthew Vines. Matthew is a young conservative, gay Christian with a high view of scripture. Vines is a well known advocate for affirming gay sexual relationship and supports gay marriage. He has a blog site and founded the advocacy group The Reformation Project.[13] He started his public work with a YouTube video on March 10, 2012, that went viral. He has posted other speeches on YouTube, and he is quoted by various mainstream media. He is a sought after speaker by various progressive Christian groups. Not only is his scholarship first-class, he folds his own Christian journey into his book. His book and advocacy are game changers. However, because of his very public profile and advocacy, Vines and his work have received a lot of criticism; much of it is negative. Although he does not have the academic credentials of some of his critics, his book utilizes resources admirably.

WHO IS DOING THE TEACHING TODAY?
ARGUING THAT HOMOSEXUALITY IS A SIN

Besides the standard commentaries that address the scriptures that reportedly proscribe homosexuality, there are those works that disagree with taking a positive stance towards homosexuality, including a magnificent piece of work published by Richard B. Hays

---

13   (http://www.reformationproject.org/)

in 1996.[14] The majority of the book relates the New Testament scriptures to the discernment of moral vision. Hays provides several examples of the interpretation of scripture providing moral direction for various contemporary dilemmas. One of those is the issue of homosexuality, which he discusses in Chapter 16.[15] Hays is a highly respected biblical scholar, and the assortment of scholars who have endorsed this book is staggering. He lines up with those traditionalists who consider the practice of homosexuality a sin regardless of the circumstances.

The most prolific, recent voice casting homosexual practice as a sin belongs to Robert A. J. Gagnon.[16] Gagnon is an associate professor of New Testament at the Pittsburgh Theological Seminary and an elder in the Presbyterian Church (USA). He holds a BA from Dartmouth and an MTS from Harvard Divinity School, as well as a PhD from the Princeton Theological Seminary. What Boswell has done for supporting the full inclusion and acceptance of homosexual activity, Gagnon has done for the polar opposite view. His thick and dense book, *The Bible and Homosexual Practice*, is an academic *tour de force* that carefully examines the biblical witness while comparing it to literature written in the same era. He elucidates cultural and religious contexts with in-depth translation analyses trying to resolve the current argument over what Paul meant by use of various words in his letter to the Corinthians. He also attempts to discount other exegetes who interpreted the scriptures as neutral and/or supportive of homosexual relationships and activity. Gagnon believes that any and all homosexual activity is a sin. Interestingly, he is more conservative than his own denomination and he is one of the younger authors that I selected.

WHY ME?

Since so much has been written on homosexuality, why write another tome? Many others have written in support of the LGBT

---

14   Hays, *Moral Vision*.
15   Hays, pp. 379-406.
16   Gagnon, *The Bible and Homosexual Practice*.

community; some are briefly introduced above. As noted, those who have had a significant relationship(s) with gay friends and/or family tend to be supportive of the LGBT community. When they exegete the scripture that has been used to oppress gays, they interpret them differently from the current negative connotations that are often introduced by words such as, "Well, the Bible says...."

So why am I writing about this subject, and in defense of the LGBT community and homosexual practice? Unlike Hamilton, Helminiak, or Rogers, I have not had an extensive ministry with the gay community. I do not have intimate relationships with any gay people who have come out of the closet. I have not witnessed committed Christian gay couples and their faithful service to the Lord. I was an engineer for about 30 years and lived in a refined bubble devoid of poverty, cultural issues like abortion or homosexuality, economic deprivation, pay-day loan sharks, lack of basic medical care, unjust immigration systems, and the like. Depending on the particular year, I mingled among PhD scientists and engineers, other university academics, or well-paid workers in a production facility.

I remember reading a *Houston Chronicle* article many years ago about the oppression of undocumented Latino workers who were not paid their wages. They had no recourse to the law because they would get deported. I remember learning about this and other injustices in the world in high resolution, but such occurrences were not in my life's sphere. I read about poverty, read about injustice of all kinds, and was partially aware of inequities in our culture. Then my world changed. I graduated in 2002 from Perkins School of Theology at Southern Methodist University with the standard preaching degree, a Masters of Divinity, at the age of 57. I was ordained an elder in the UMC at the age of 60. At first, my appointments were as an associate at churches with relatively well-to-do congregants. My refined bubble was burst by pastoral ministry with a more diverse group of people, but the upper middle class nature of the parishes was not all that different from my previous environment. In 2004 I was appointed pastor of a church in the county seat of a rural and poverty-stricken county of Texas. People tend to think of Texas as cattle and oil and money, but none of those is prominent in our town. There is no industry, jobs, or government-provided safety net. We have been abandoned by offices that once included social security, SNAP (food stamps), medical care for the indigent, employment assistance, aid for the aging and disabled, and the like. People are without much recourse.

On September 23, 2005, our town and surrounding community were hit hard by Hurricane Rita. Since we were a rural area, and New Orleans was still reeling from Katrina, we were pretty much ignored by state and federal governments and agencies. Our city and county governments did a yeoman's job of putting back the pieces, but many, many people suffered for a long time. I had the distinct honor and privilege of helping host the Mennonite Disaster Service (MDS) that provided enormous help in rebuilding homes damaged by the hurricane. However, after the first few weeks of reviewing damage and starting projects, these legendary servants of Christ were confounded. Their mission was to restore homes to pre-hurricane condition; that is, to fix the damage from Rita. There were a lot of damaged roofs, but when they stripped the shingles and plywood, they found that entire houses had pre-existing structural damage from years of zero maintenance and/or initial substandard construction. MDS resolved this issue at the management level and started rebuilding houses as needed. Over the years they even built a lot of new homes for the economically disadvantaged of our community.

The last vestiges of my previous life exploded early in the rebuilding process when we visited a woman whose home had some hurricane damage. She also showed us a bathroom problem. The wax seal around her commode had been leaking for an extended period of time and the floor around it was rotted and the commode halfway fallen through the floor. That is bad, but what we observed next was worse. The drain underneath the commode was not connected and, when it was used, the waste simply went under the house that was up on concrete blocks. Since that day I have observed people living without running water, electricity, air conditioning, heating, furniture, and so forth. This is reality in parts of America. What does this have to do with homosexuality? There is a great amount of potential ministerial time wasted on fighting a hot-button issue like gay marriage when there are so many needs that the scriptures teach us to address in an active way. People are going hungry; people are homeless; the gap between the rich and everybody else keeps expanding; we have substandard medical care for the poor; our mental health system sucks; food stamps (SNAP) were cut recently; the minimum wage is far removed from a living wage; and social justice in America is in the pits.

We are all too familiar with the divorce rates and collapse of heterosexual marriage. I actually dislike doing many weddings because I can tell that the focus is on the wedding and not the marriage. Virtually all couples who are getting married are already living together, and many are living together (we used to call this shacking up) without any benefit or thought of ever getting married. Heterosexual commitment is disappearing. In my own parish, single mothers with children are common, and fathers are not supplying any financial support. Sexual violence against women is widespread. A recent article in *Time* magazine highlighted the epidemic of rape in university campuses across the US,[17] where the extreme assault problem makes college the most unsafe place for young women to be, and these are heterosexual acts of violence towards women. What is the church teaching our young men as they are growing up? The church's responses to heteroeroticism may not create a great amount of controversy, but our responses are woefully inadequate.

One of my motivators is the church's lack of emphasis on what we should be doing as a church and individual Christians. There are Christian works being done, but how much more ministry could we do if we were not as concerned with boundaries as the Pharisees were in Jesus' time.

---

17   *Time* magazine, May 26, 2014, pp. 20-29.

Another motivator is my acquired understanding of human nature that leads to scapegoating. From 30 years in the secular, business world I learned that people try to feel good about themselves by putting others down. Stuck in a boring job with an overbearing boss and little room for self-esteem or hope, people tend to elevate themselves psychologically by playing on the foibles of others. This may require the metaphoric knife in the back, a subtle dig, a bit of one-sided gossip, or just watching with enjoyment as someone else slowly twists in the wind... hung up by the idiosyncrasies of the working environment. When this put-down of others becomes directed at a minority group, it becomes scapegoating: "It's not our fault that the project failed, it was those bean counters. They screw up everything we try to do!" I think that our culture and the church have been involved in scapegoating the LGBT community.

I grew up in a fundamentalist church. During a formative time in my life, I heard a disproportionate number of sermons on the evil of alcohol consumption. I was a teetotaler so I could feel pretty smug about myself on the railroad to heaven. By focusing our energy on the LGBT community we can hide our sins from ourselves by heaping hot coals on the heads a minority that certainly does not deserve the derision and oppression they have received. Then there are those who turn honestly to the Bible to discern the very few scriptures that seem to relate to homosexuality, and that is why I am focused on the scripture and what others have written about the scriptures.

The Bible has at least 168 texts that relate to the common good, social justice, and the care of others. The Bible is replete with admonitions of loving one another and accepting Christ as our savior. Our savior spent his earthly life addressing suffering, hunger, disabilities, forgiveness, love, and teaching about the wealth gap between the rich and the poor. We tend to sweep those aside as we scapegoat the gay community. The Bible also has nine texts that have been interpreted to castigate the LGBT community. At the very least, the conventional interpretations of these texts are highly questionable! My thesis is that we need to get this divisive red-herring out of the way and turn to our Christ-given mission of loving one another. However, we are going to have a difficult time getting through the issue of homosexuality as long as we adopt polar opposite interpretations of the scripture. One way to bring us to together is to broaden the subject to human sexuality ... that includes all of us. We are all sexual beings and our sexual behaviors are moral issues. Some sexual behaviors affect only us as individuals and/or couples and some sexual behaviors affect society. We are all fallible human beings, but scriptures can lead us to better synthesis of our sexuality without disparaging and scapegoating the LGBT community.

A detailed analysis of the various exegetical resources would be tedious at best and boring at worst. Hence, for each clobber text, I adhere to the following format: the text from the NRSV; an overview of the text itself; a brief summary of the salient points from the detailed analysis; and finally, an extensive "exegetical analysis" using the various sources from authors discussed earlier. The reader could easily skip over or skim the detailed analysis and still understand what the exegetical results are.

PART 1: WHAT DO THE SO-CALLED CLOBBER VERSES TEACH ABOUT HOMOSEXUALITY

Part 1A: The Old Testament Clobber Verses

Sexuality in the Genesis Creation Stories

1) Genesis 1:26 *Then God said, "Let us make humankind in our image, according to our likeness; and let them have dominion over the fish of the sea, and over the birds of the air, and over the cattle, and over all the wild animals of the earth, and over every creeping thing that creeps upon the earth." *[27]* So God created humankind in his image, in the image of God he created them; male and female he created them. *[28]* God blessed them, and God said to them, "Be fruitful and multiply, and fill the earth and subdue it; and have dominion over the fish of the sea and over the birds of the air and over every living thing that moves upon the earth." *[29]* God said, "See, I have given you every plant yielding seed that is upon the face of all the earth, and every tree with seed in its fruit; you shall have them for food. *[30]* And to every beast of the earth, and to every bird of the air, and to everything that creeps on the earth, everything that has the breath of life, I have given every green plant for food." And it was so. *[31]* God saw everything that he had made, and indeed, it was very good. And there was evening and there was morning, the sixth day.*

2) Genesis 2:24 *Therefore a man leaves his father and his mother and clings to his wife, and they become one flesh. *[25]* And the man and his wife were both naked, and were not ashamed.*

There is always the argument made that because homosexuality is excluded from discussion in Genesis, and since only the heterosexual relationship is ordained, then homosexual relationship is precluded. Let us consider a similar text on a different subject as an example of the illogic of this position:

Genesis 3:23 *therefore the LORD God sent him forth from the garden of Eden, to till the ground from which he was taken.*

Most readers are familiar with the original sin of Adam and Eve and their expulsion from the garden. One of the several results of their expulsion and punishment is the necessity of work. No more easy life in the garden that provided everything for their needs; we would have to work for our daily bread as a result of their disobedience and arrogance. The consequences of and salvation from sin is what the Bible and church is about, but we are considering only this narrow scripture. Adam and Eve were sent forth to till the ground. Their lives would be fraught with sweat and tears as they farmed the earth to grow food to eat. The text does not mention butchers, bakers, or candlestick makers. Since other professions are not mentioned, are they condemned? After all, God said to till the land not to code computer programs. This seems silly but it is the same argument put forth for condemning homosexuality because of its absence in Genesis.

Most ancient cultures had some kind of creation myth or myths in an attempt to explain how their particular culture came into being. Most are at least partially *etiological*, attempts to understand why "we" are the way we are and why the world around us exists as it does. The earliest cultures that we have any records of illustrate our ability to transcend our daily foibles and question our own existence and thoughts. The primitive myths tried to explain the existence of the sun, moon, stars, our own land, rivers, rain, water, animals, fish, plants, and the like. Questions about our relationship with our creator(s), each other, what kind of people we are, what is right and wrong, and so forth, required the ability to ponder our own thought processes and actions. The creation stories (there are two) in Genesis have some parallels with other creation myths, perhaps even using some of them in crafting what has become the Israelite, Jewish, and Christian biblical accounts, the first narrative appearing in Genesis 1:1-2:4a and the second appearing in Genesis 2:4b-3:24.

There are several things that make the Israelite myth radically different from other ancient creation myths. The anthropology, theology, relational covenant, and nature of humankind standout as major, awesome content even if some more ancient elements remain. Firstly, there is only one God. The Yahwist cult and the formation of Judaism became monotheist; there were struggles with belief in other gods and idols documented in the First Testament, but they morphed into monotheism. Secondly, God cannot be represented by any image whatsoever. God is the unseen, transcendent, all powerful God who speaks the world into being. Thirdly, God is involved with the world even if he is not part of the world. He comes down into the world to create humankind, like a potter creates a vessel, and shares in the lives of his creatures. God is not capricious in playing games with his creatures as depicted in other myths. Fourthly, God created humankind in his own image (*imago Dei*) and pronounced us "very good." We were created "good," but given the freedom to choose between accepting, obeying, and loving God in return, or not. Adam and Eve chose wrongly, resulting in estrangement from God. The *imago Dei* is an overarching theme of Creation and the revelation of the Bible. This theme has nothing to do with sexual orientation. God created us all: different races, different ethnicities, different colors, and different sexual orientations.

The creation itself is quite amazing as told by the two narratives. There is no real "how" or "when" in the creation. How God does what he does is not as important as the theological content or "why" God does what God does. Although God creates the world *ex nihilo* or out of nothing, there is an ordering of things that goes on, a separation of the light from darkness and separation of water from dry land. God is putting things in their places where each belongs. One of the overarching themes of the first narrative is the "order" or "structure" of creation. Not so much the chronological order as the order made of things; plants grown on the land, animals that creep and cattle, fish that swim in the sea, and so forth. There is order to God's creation, an order that will evolve or be consistent with laws regarding the mixing of things such as two types of cloth, cheese and meat, or two crops in the same field. Similarly, dietary or Kosher laws will regulate the types of things that can or cannot be eaten. Things from water should have scales and creatures without scales, like shrimp or oysters, will be impure, un-Kosher, or an abomination. Animals without the cloven hoof that do not eat the cud are unclean, such as pigs. They are out of the order of things. These concepts of order and structure play a big role in understanding many of the laws in Leviticus and other precepts in the First Testament.

The creation myth narratives do not mention homosexuality, but they do not condemn it. They also do not mention polygamy, which was practiced by the patriarchs in the Bible with little negative verbiage. Abraham had two wives, and Jacob had four wives. The later kings had numerous wives. Perhaps the negative commentary is given by how much trouble and extreme dysfunction occurred in the families with multiple wives. Sarah and Hagar had serious conflict, resulting in Hagar being banished to die in the wilderness with her son Ishmael, only to be rescued by God himself. The wives of Jacob, Rachel and Leah, although sisters, were envious of each other and fought for Jacob's attention and affection. Of course, David and Bathsheba is a well-known story, and Solomon began the destruction of the united kingdom with his countless number of wives and concubines. There is a trajectory in biblical understanding that is illustrated by our rejection (for the most part) of polygamy. It is immoral even though practiced in the Bible. Context changes over the years, and our interpretation changes with context.

The exegetical points are the following:

- ✓ The command to procreate is contextual and not a moral, eternal truth.
- ✓ Just because homosexual relationships are not mentioned in the creation narratives does not infer that they are immoral.

✓   Sexual orientation is God-given, not a choice.

✓   The argument about "created or natural fittedness of penis and vagina" is not based on biblical warrants. Biology does not determine biblical, moral truths.

✓   To be created in God's image has nothing to do with sexuality; we are created for intimate relationship with God and each other.

✓   To literally read the creation narratives as excluding homosexual relationship is to denigrate the beauty and depth of their meaning. We are all created in the image of God regardless of race, color, sex, and sexual orientation.

✓   Beginning with the creation narrative and expressed throughout scripture is the importance of covenantal relationships between God's children. The creation narratives should be read more broadly with an emphasis on all divine and human relationships whether sexual or nonsexual. Relationship commitments are tantamount to divine-human relationships. Homosexual relationships are not precluded.

EXEGETICAL ANALYSIS

Alexander notes the dramatically different context now versus then. The command to procreate may have made sense when more children were needed to fight wars with surrounding enemies of the Israelites, "But what about now? Do we continue to take seriously God's charge that we be fruitful and multiply in an age that is marked by severe overpopulation and a serious shortage of safe drinking water, and in which thousands of children die *every day* of starvation?"[18] What Alexander basically is assuming is that the command to procreate was situational or contextual rather than an eternal, moral truth.

Some of the texts in Genesis have been used to preach against the attribute and/or practice of homosexuality. Since the creation

---

18   Alexander, p. 26.

scriptures only talk about procreation (be fruitful and multiply), and Adam and Eve are a heterosexual couple, some Bible readers have essentially concluded that only heterosexual couples are "created good" and homosexuals must be, by comparison, "bad." Gagnon uses the absence of homosexuality in Genesis as the locus of his argument throughout his book. Gagnon's introduction begins (emphasis mine), "Having established that the biblical texts that speak directly to the issue of same-sex intercourse express unambiguous opposition to it and do so in large part on the credible grounds of the anatomical, procreative, and interpersonal *complementarity* of male and females ...."[19] In other words, Gagnon is arguing that heterosexual union produces offspring and the penis and vagina fit together. In a detailed review of early Judaism, Gagnon makes the argument that homosexuality is contrary to nature, or *para physin* in the Greek, instead of in accordance with nature, or *kata physin*. He makes constant reference to penis and vagina "fittedness" and/or "complementarity." As I mentioned in the introduction, this fittedness, even when expressed more eloquently, is no different from the Duck Dynasty position.

Gagnon provides a detailed and sweeping analysis of early Judaism (200 BCE to 200 CE) that adds significant warrants to his conclusions.[20] Judaism, unlike the Greco-Roman culture, admonished male same-sex eroticism. The various writings that he quotes as declaring prohibition to homoeroticism presumably do so with gender complementarity as the root reason for the prohibition. Gagnon dismisses attempts by others to support homoeroticism in our society based on the supposition that scripture and Judaism only outlawed pederasty and cultic temple prostitution rather than homoeroticism in general.

For Gagnon, all fulfillment of homosexuality is a sin; hence, homosexual orientation is not a sin, but those with such an orientation must remain celibate. According to Gagnon, there are no exceptions: God created male and female and put them together

---

19   Gagnon, p. 40 of introduction.
20   Gagnon, Chapter 2.

to fill the earth with people; man and wife cling together as one; there are no alternatives.

Gagnon argues that even with a gay orientation, the only possible recourse is to become celibate. Yet, "sexual orientation is part of someone's nature and may be just as God-given as heterosexuality."[21] So the entire argument of natural law (what is according to nature versus what is against nature) is not valid; something that is God-given cannot be unnatural or against nature.

Hays has very little to say about the creation stories in Genesis, but rather takes their interpretations as a given:

> From Genesis 1 onward, Scripture affirms repeatedly that God made man and woman for one another and that our sexual desires rightly find fulfillment within heterosexual marriage…This normative canonical picture of marriage provides the positive backdrop against which the Bible's few emphatic negations of homosexuality must be read.[22]

For Hays, as well as Gagnon, the interpretations of the biblical creation stories are the fundamental truth of prohibiting homosexual relationships of all kinds. Their reading of Genesis 1 and 2 is pretty much what is read or heard in less academic circles: "God created Adam and Eve, not Adam and Steve." According to this thinking, God created man and woman for monogamous marriage, and there are no exceptions to God's creationary intent.

Not very many exegetes actually bother to refute the anti-homosexual interpretations taken from the creation story. Jack Rogers does not explicitly quote the Genesis stories of creation, but he refutes the "natural law" that is expressed so well by Gagnon: "He [Gagnon] goes on to say that the Old Testament Holiness Code 'was responding to the conviction that same-sex intercourse was fundamentally incompatible with the creation of men and women as anatomically complementary sexual beings.'"[23] Recalling Gagnon's idea of the fittedness of penis and vagina, Rogers is noting

---

21 Rogers. p. 79.
22 Hays, p. 390.
23 Rogers, p. 78.

that Gagnon is more dependent on non-biblical warrants rather than scripture. Once one decides that only penis-and-vagina sexual expression is valid based on anatomical considerations, the biblical narratives are interpreted through that lens of presupposition.

Mark Allan Powell, in a compendium published by the Evangelical Lutheran Church in America (ELCA), provides a balanced and cautious view of the "natural" versus "unnatural" terms used to describe heterosexual versus homosexual activity. He concedes that we might rightly prefer the two terms (natural and unnatural) vis-à-vis the "be fruitful and multiply" of Genesis 1:28. Indeed the narrative does establish a family-oriented order for generation after generation as two parents of opposite sex produce and raise children to continue the process. However, he points out that the Bible does not automatically declare what is contrary to "natural" as being immoral, and he notes the following accepted exceptions:[24]

✓ Abraham, Jacob, David, Solomon, and other biblical characters had more than one wife.
✓ Those heterosexual couples that are childless, for whatever reason, are not regarded as immoral.
✓ The church does recognize and allow divorce and remarriage.
✓ Some people (Paul and Jesus for example) have chosen singleness and celibacy. They are not considered immoral because they produce no children

According to Powell, hypothetically there is the possibility of the church recognizing some homosexual relationships; however, he does not use the term "marriage" of homosexuals.

When we ask the question whether homosexuality is a sin or not, we need to ask the same question about heterosexuality. The Bible has a lot to say about heterosexuality and very little about homosexuality. Many read "they become one flesh" as a condemnation of homosexuality because it refers to men and women getting married and/or having sexual intercourse. The word "marry" is

---

24   Childs, *Faithful Conversations*, pp. 21-22.

not mentioned explicitly, but certainly implies a committed relationship between a man and woman. Sex is a gift within that relationship. Yet, the language of "one flesh" is not a only a reference to sexual relationships per se; it is a term describing a deep, covenantal relationship.[25]

Homosexual relationships are not mentioned. However, if we consider that content of the text, along with the fact that Jesus quoted this very text within the context of divorce (Matthew 19:4-9 and Mark 10:6-12), this text is about commitment within a heterosexual relationship; yet, many who use it as a proof text for the condemnation of homosexuality have ignored what it is really about. As a society and a church we have condemned homosexuality but have little or nothing to say about the biblical command for committed heterosexual relationship. This is not a treatise on divorce, living together without the benefit of commitment, casual sex, or serial polygamy (my term for multiple marriages), but God's will for sexual relationship is one of commitment. The church has wasted a lot of effort on condemning homosexuality but has avoided condemning the sexual actions of the base that provides the tithe. It is much easier to scapegoat a minority than address the sins of the majority.

In a very detailed linguistic analysis of the Genesis creation stories, Lings notes that the language in 2:21-25 refers to a radically intimate relationship between God's creatures. Sexual language and connotations are missing. This was radical in that era because women were not valued as partners in the relationship, and it was and is radical because it ordains a covenantal commitment to each other.[26]

Perhaps the church should spend more time helping to build healthy, viable, Christian relationships than condemning LGBT relationships.

Victor Paul Furnish writes about the moral teaching of Paul rather than the First Testament. However, since Paul was a Pharisee, a First Testament scholar, he was deeply influenced by First Testa-

---

25   Vines, pp. 144-148.
26   Lings, pp. 3-43.

ment writing. Therefore, Furnish does discuss some First Testament writings on our subject of homosexuality that might have impacted Paul's position. Furnish notes that Verses 2:20-24, in the second creation narrative, do not refer to sexual activity or procreation. Woman is created as a helper or companion with no distinguishing sexual characteristics. Rather, what makes her a fit companion is that she is "bone of [his] bones and flesh of [his] flesh." Both accounts are etiological in that they define why things are the way they are or the way they are assumed to be. They do not contain any language that is ethical or moral in genre or content. Furnish asserts, "These accounts provide no scriptural basis for the claim, frequently made, that homosexuality is inherently and unconditionally evil because it is a perversion of the created order."[27]

So what does Genesis have to do with homosexuality? Not much, if anything. God does ordain heterosexual practice as the mechanism for maintaining the species. The same is true for the animal and plant kingdoms in total. All are somewhat different but the ongoingness of a species depends on replication of itself or else it disappears. Whilst this may seem to be the "natural" way for things to work, that is not always the case. Homosexual activity has been documented among hundreds of species of animals. There are several reasons why "be fruitful and multiply" cannot be an exclusionary statement for homosexual activity:

✓ It implies that sex is only for procreation. That would exclude sex for folks beyond the childbearing ages, couples that cannot have children, individuals who are sterile, couples who decide not to have children, singles who are celibate, or people who like sex. Are people without children outside the blessings of God? Are they immoral?

✓ How fruitful is fruitful? When this was written there was a genuine need to produce many children to keep Israelite people fecund. They could have disappeared as a people. If this were a moral commandment, it would be better

---

27   Furnish, p. 66.

defined. Should I have 4, 6, 8 or how many children are necessary and commanded?

✓ Large families have been necessary in agrarian and hunter/gatherer cultures, but the earth is now overcrowded in some places. Many countries are kept underdeveloped because they have too many births.

With a focus that seeks to prove a predetermined position (homosexuality is sinful) we can miss many other important truths in this scripture. Besides the command to "be fruitful and multiply," we are commanded to subdue the earth and have dominion over other created beings. This raises a lot of questions that are beyond the scope of this writing: 1) what is our responsibility for climate change that is impacting creation? 2) what do we owe endangered species? 3) what is our role in creation of our environment? And so forth.

The crowning glory of the creation story is the combination of "very good" and "in God's image" or the *imago Dei*. These address what we are like, what our relationship with God is, and what God's intent or vision is for his creation and creatures. We are inherently good. Our creation is "very good" (1:31), and Adam and Eve were created sinless by God; Adam from the earth and Eve from Adam's side. Humankind is created in God's own image! There are many attempts to explicate the meaning of the short phrase *imago Dei*. It does not mean that we look like God or God looks like us. God is not a sexual being like we are. He/she is not an old man with a long beard sitting on a throne in the heavens. To Christians, God is Trinity, but that is not a part of the understanding of the writer(s) of Genesis 1. What makes us "like" God? Unlike the rest of God's creatures we have the ability to love if we so choose. God created us with the ability to love him and each other. As moral, contingent agents we have the freedom to make real choices; good ones and bad ones. We were created with a special covenant between us, God, and each other. Unfortunately, the first mythological characters broke the covenant, and the power of sin entered the world along with the goodness created with God. The message is that God created us with the ability to make decisions and love him, but sin is powerful, and we make bad (sinful) choices.

The "be fruitful and multiply" phrase that appears in 1:26-28 merely establishes the male/female biological relationship that exists with the rest of God's creation. There is nothing ethical or moral with respect to this designation. Rather, the important ethical/moral statement is that we are made in God's image. This defines us relationally to God and each other as unique from the rest of creation.

Of course, getting hung up on literal phrases such as "be fruitful and multiply" obscures the beauty and ultimate truth of Chapter 1 in Genesis. The essence of this short paragraph about humankind creation is that we are created in God's image, and that God pronounces our creation "very good." This anthropological view of creation is the center of salvific doctrine: 1) we were created in God's very image so our relationship to God was intended to be very personal and close; 2) our basic, created, human nature is good, we are innately good, our bodies, sexuality, and very being is good and not something to hide or be ashamed of; 3) there is no subjugation order of the sexes in this text, and God created male and female in his image; 4) there is no race bias in God's created order, all people are created in God's image. This is not even close to complete discussion of salvation theology or anthropology but serves only to explicate what we might miss by seeking to prove a predetermined doctrine (proof texting). To read defamation of homosexuality into this text is to do an injustice to the holy word of God.

SODOMY FROM SODOM AND GOMORRAH

3) Genesis 19:4 *But before they lay down, the men of the city, the men of Sodom, both young and old, all the people to the last man, surrounded the house;* [5] *and they called to Lot, "Where are the men who came to you tonight? Bring them out to us, so that we may know them."*

The recent, traditional interpretation of this text is so widespread that it has linguistically and morally shaped our culture. The cities of Sodom and Gomorrah were both destroyed by God in a long narrative that appears in Genesis (the entire story is included in Genesis 18:16-19:29).

God says to Abraham: "How great is the outcry against Sodom and Gomorrah and how very grave their sin! I must go down and see whether they have done altogether according to the outcry that has come to me; and if not, I will know."[28]

Abraham intervenes for the city, and God promises that if at least 10 people are not living in sin, he will spare the cities. So God sends two angels down to the town of Sodom to destroy it with fire as punishment for this very grave sin. When the angels arrive, the man Lot, who is Abraham's nephew, extends hospitality to them by bringing then into his home and feeding them. The people of the town respond as noted above; the entire male population tries to take the two angels by force and "know them." They would have gained entry except the angels strike the men blind, and Lot and his daughters escape as the town is destroyed by fire from God. Lot's wife looks back and is turned into a pillar of salt.

To "know them" is a commonly accepted biblical euphemism for sexual penetration, so the consensus interpretation is that the sin of Sodom (and Gomorrah) is homosexuality, and specifically male-male anal sex. The men of the town gathered to rape the two angels via anal sex. This common interpretation has resulted in the words "sodomy" to denote male-male anal sex and "sodomite" to denote males that practice anal sex. Since God punished the town of Sodom by destroying it with fire, it has been assumed that God has mandated a strong moral disfavor of male-male anal sex, a moral sin that is so abhorrent to God that he would destroy a whole city with fire for the practice.

The exegetical points are the following:

✓ The command "to know" the strangers does not necessarily

---

28   Genesis 18:20b-21. God speaking directly to his chosen one, Abraham.

refer to sexual activity. The Hebrew is not conclusive.

✓ If same-sex intercourse is intended, it would be rape, not sexual consent. Consensual homosexual intercourse is not mentioned in this text.

✓ The text includes all males in the town. If all of the males were truly homosexuals, as we understand homosexuality, there would be no town, because there would be no children produced.

✓ The sins of Sodom included inhospitality, injustice, pride, gluttony, indifference to the needy, lies, greed, luxury, heterosexual abuse.

✓ This text has absolutely nothing to do with consensual homoeroticism.

EXEGETICAL ANALYSIS

Gagnon is, once again, the quintessential advocate for the biblical interpretation that all homoerotic behavior is sinful. As we shall find in subsequent biblical exegesis by Gagnon, he always draws upon certain suppositions about unnatural homosexual behavior versus natural heterosexual behavior:

> Just as one form of illicit copulation (between angels and women) contributed to the earlier cataclysm of the great flood in Genesis 6 (an important element in the general "wickedness of humankind," 6:5) so too another form of unnatural sexual relations (between men) served as a key contributing factor in the cataclysmic destruction of Sodom and Gomorrah.[29]

In a long discourse on the so-called "sin of Sodom," Gagnon does acknowledge homosexual rape (as opposed to consensual intercourse) as the intent of the men of Sodom. He also analyzes various biblical texts (discussed below) that refer to the sin of Sodom and Gomorrah as inhospitality and social injustice in Ezekiel,

---

29   Gagnon, p.75.

Isaiah, Matthew, Luke, and Jude.[30] Gagnon does recognize the contexts of inhospitality and social injustice that appear in these texts, and he admits the element of rape as opposed to consensual sexual intercourse, yet he still contends for the generalization of homoeroticism as at least one of the sins of Sodom. He notes Jesus' reference to Sodom and Gomorrah in Matthew and Luke, and Gagnon draws the following conclusion.

> … Sodom is singled out as the most atrocious example of inhospitality mentioned in the scriptures of Israel (a reasonable interpretation given the cataclysmic judgment of God on the city). What made it so atrocious? Many factors, to be sure, but the height of the town's evil was epitomized by the attempt to rape visiting strangers and a resident alien, and worse still, sexual intercourse with males: emasculating Lot's guests by treating them not in accordance with their natures as males but as females to be penetrated in anal sex….[31]

These texts will be discussed below vis-à-vis those who argue against the broad generalization that all homoerotic activity is sinful. Gagnon acknowledges that the main elements that argue against a broad generalization—that it was homosexual rape and not consensual sex, and that the sin of Sodom and Gomorrah was social injustice/inhospitality—and yet he still generalizes the narrative on the basis of "their natures as male." This argument is particularly weak. All readers of scripture would agree that homosexual rape is abusive, violent, and highly sinful, but many would argue that does not include all homoeroticism.

The other major player in the argument for considering homosexual conduct a sin is Hays. Interestingly, he does not find anything in the narrative of the destruction of Sodom to hang his hat on: "Indeed, there is nothing in the rest of the biblical tradition,

---

30 Isaiah 1:7-17, Ezekiel 16:49-50, Matthew 10:14-15, Luke 10:10-12, and Jude 7.
31 Gagnon, p. 91.

save an obscure reference in Jude 7, to suggest that the sin of Sodom was particularly identified with sexual misconduct of any kind."[32]

Robert Alter, in his commentary on Genesis, does not dwell on the events at the door of Lot's house in Sodom except to refer to the citizens' intentions of "homosexual gang rape."[33] Alter is one of the premier language experts. If he says "to know" means intercourse, that conclusion carries a lot of weight. Brueggemann notes that the popular interpretation of this text is generally taken as a desire for homosexual relations; hence the words "sodomy" and "sodomites." If so, it is not about general homosexual relations but "gang rape." He follows that exegesis with this revelation:

> However, the Bible gives considerable evidence that the sin of Sodom was not specifically sexual, but a general disorder of a society organized against God. Thus in Isaiah 1:9, 3:9, the reference to injustice; in Jeremiah 23:14, to a variety of irresponsible acts which are named; and in Ezekiel 16:49 the sin is pride, excessive food, and indifference to the needy... that issue is presented in a way scarcely pertinent to contemporary discussions of homosexuality.[34]

Fretheim, in the *New Interpreter's Bible*, arrives at a similar position as Brueggemann:

> The text *illustrates* the situation in Sodom as homosexual activity... but refers to the abusive violence and savage inhospitality. The text does not talk about homosexual activity or orientation generally, or nonviolent sexual behavior. Other biblical references to Sodom lift up a wide variety of behavior, from neglect of the poor and needy to lies, greed, luxury, heterosexual abuse, and inhospitality to strangers (Isaiah 1:9-10; Jeremiah 23:14; Lamentations 4:6; Ezekiel 16:48-55; Zephaniah 2:9). Jesus remains true to the text in condemning a town to a fate like Sodom's because of its refusal to receive strangers who bear the word of God (Matthew 10:14-15; 11:23-24;

---

32   Hays, p. 381.
33   Alter, p, 85.
34   Brueggemann, p. 164.

Luke 10:12; 17:29; 2 Peter 2:8; only in Jude 7 does the reference to homosexual behavior possibly become explicit).[35]

Furnish, in his text on the *Moral Teaching of Paul,* agrees with the other neutral exegetes, Brueggemann, Fretheim, and Alter: "This is not a story about homosexual behavior in general, and certainly not a story about homosexual acts performed by consenting adults in a committed, loving, relationship."[36] He recounts the sins of Sodom and Gomorrah that are contained elsewhere in scripture that have already been revealed by Fretheim and Brueggemann.

Our first inclusionist, J. Neil Alexander, spills quite a bit of ink on the story of the destruction of Sodom and provides several interpretations of the activity of the men at the door of Lot. One interpretation is that the men want "to know" the men in a totally non-sexual way. Hospitality was a crucial and urgent demand in that culture, and Lot, who was a sojourner himself, had usurped that responsibility and privilege from the townspeople. Considering the sexual content of Lot's offer to give up his daughters to the angry mob, that interpretation seems unlikely. Alexander is much more comfortable with the contention that the action of the men of the village would have been gang rape rather that consensual same-sex relations. As with other commentators he notes the use of the word "outcry" in verse 13: "For we are about to destroy this place, because the outcry against its people has become great before the Lord, and the Lord has sent us to destroy it." The word outcry usually refers to sins that violate God's justice. This interpretation matches other references in scripture that refer to Sodom:

> ...a veritable laundry list of things that God finds displeasing: spiritual apathy and casualness (Isaiah 1:9-10); adultery and lying (Jeremiah, Chapter 14); those who feast when children are hungry (Lamentations 4:5-6); haughtiness, pride, excess food, prosperous ease, failure to support the poor and needy (Ezekiel 16:48-55)...Jesus says that a town that fails to welcome the stranger—those who are sent to us in the

---

35   Fretheim, p. 477.
36   Furnish, p. 59.

name of Jesus—will suffer the same fate as Sodom (Matthew
10:14-15, 11:23-24; Luke 10:12; 17:29).

The early inclusionist Boswell takes a different tack in his interpretation of the narrative of the destruction of Sodom. Since he
notes the various references to the sins of Sodom as expressed in
other scriptures in the Bible, he doubts that the men of the town
are even threatening sex with the angels at all:

> Briefly put, the thesis of this trend in scholarship is that
> Lot was violating the custom of Sodom (where he was him-
> self not a citizen but a "sojourner") by entertaining unknown
> guests within the city walls at night without obtaining per-
> mission of the elders of the city. When the men of Sodom
> gathered around to demand that the strangers be brought out
> to them, "that they might *know* them," they meant no more
> than to "know" who they were, and the city was consequently
> destroyed not for sexual immorality but for the sin of inhos-
> pitality to strangers.[37]

Lings agrees with Boswell and Alexander on the translation
and meaning of the Hebrew word *yada* (to know). In a very lengthy
and detailed linguistic and literary analysis, he convincingly makes
the argument that the men of the village are there to interrogate
the visitors who are staying with Lot.[38]

Indeed, there is an element of inhospitality in this narrative,
but I am not convinced that sexual attack was not what the men
were up to. To assault them was the ultimate inhospitable event.
Boswell is the first to point out the apocryphal references, as well as
canonical scripture, that list the sins of Sodom as radically different
from what has been assumed in modern times. The attachment
of the words sodomy and sodomites to male anal sex and those
who practice the same is an extremely poor rendering of the text.
According to Boswell, if sex is involved at all it is an expression of
extreme inhospitality.

---

37   Boswell, *Christianity*, p. 95.
38   Lings, pp. 79-119.

Helminiak presents several possible interpretations to the narrative of Sodom: 1) the villagers were angry with Lot because he usurped their privilege of offering hospitality, 2) they simply wanted to know what the two strangers were doing in town, 3) they were angry with Lot for extending hospitality to strangers, 4) there were sexual intents among the villagers, but such action would represent male-male rape and sexual abuse not consensual sex, and 5) in other biblical scriptures, early church patriarchs refer to a plethora of sins in Sodom unrelated to homosexuality. Since Jesus recognized the sin of Sodom as inhospitality, "those who oppress homosexuals because of the supposed 'sin of Sodom' may themselves be the real 'sodomites,' as the Bible understands it."[39]

Powell makes short work of both the Sodom narrative and the following Judges narrative about the Levite's concubine: "The stories speak only of the sin of homosexual rape and say nothing at all about consensual relations between persons of the same sex."[40]

Countryman also dismisses both of the Sodom and Levite's concubine narratives as containing homosexual elements: "Neither story, as it stands in scripture, condemns same-gender sexual intercourse as such; violence against strangers is the point."[41]

Rogers also spends little time on the Sodom narrative or Levite's concubine narratives: "The best available scholarship shows that these texts have nothing to do with homosexuality as such."[42] Homosexual rape was often perpetrated by the victors of a battle to manifest their superiority over the vanquished. Anal sex was a means of treating a man like a woman, which in a very patriarchal culture was very degrading for the man. That is why Lot offered his daughters to the villagers: protecting a man from being degraded as a woman was more important that protecting his own daughters. Women were treated as chattel. So this proposed attack is a gender issue, not a sexual issue.

---

39   Helminiak, p. 50.
40   Powell, p. 23.
41   Countryman, p. 25.
42   Rogers, p. 67.

The contemporary, consensus opinion from the larger population of church members and even clergy is that this biblical event exemplifies the moral issue or sin of homosexual practice. Many believe that Sodom was destroyed because the men of Sodom were engaged in homosexual practices, that the intent to have sex with the two strangers, who happened to be angels, was just an expression of their common practice of male-male sexual intercourse. If that were the case, the town would have ceased to exist! The Bible says that every single male in the town came to Lot's door. If they were all homosexuals, there would be no procreation, and the town would have died. Lot offered his daughters to the angry crowd in place of the two men, which is an action that implicates the extremely low value placed upon women and the radical protection afforded the men under Lot's hospitality values. Since he offered his daughters, the men were obviously heterosexuals intending upon raping the two strangers. Since they were heterosexuals desiring to rape what they thought were men, then we should consider that immoral, sinful behavior because it would be an abusive, violent attack on the persons of the angels.

THE RAPE OF THE LEVITE'S CONCUBINE

4)   Judges 19:22 *While they were enjoying themselves, the men of the city, a perverse lot, surrounded the house, and started pounding on the door. They said to the old man, the master of the house, "Bring out the man who came into your house, so that we may have intercourse with him."* [23] *And the man, the master of the house, went out to them and said to them, "No, my brothers, do not act so wickedly. Since this man is my guest, do not do this vile thing.* [24] *Here are my virgin daughter and his concubine; let me bring them out now. Ravish them and do whatever you want to them; but against this man do not do such a vile thing."* [25] *But the men would not listen to him. So the man seized his concubine, and put her out to them. They wantonly raped her, and abused her all through the night until the morning. And as the dawn began to break, they let her go.*

This story sounds somewhat like the story of Lot and Sodom, and it does start out in a very similar fashion. However, it ends up as a bizarre story about the death of the concubine and a war between the tribes over the death of the concubine even though her husband is culpable. A certain Levite (unnamed) living in the remote hill country of Ephraim has a concubine that comes from Bethlehem in Judah. She becomes angry with the Levite and returns to her father's house in Bethlehem. After four months the Levite decides to go to her and entice her to return with him. The concubine's father welcomes the Levite, and they eat and drink together for days. Each time the Levite prepares to leave, the father gives him more food and drink until it is too late to depart. Finally the Levite, concubine, servant, and two donkeys leave, but it is, indeed, late in the day, and they must stop in Gibeah, a city in the tribe of Benjamin. The small entourage goes to the town square in hopes of being offered respite for the night. After some time had passed, an old man coming in from the fields takes them home and attends to their needs. The old man was from Ephraim, and hence, a sojourner like Lot.

Just as in the Sodom story, the men of the town show up demanding sex with the Levite. There were no angels in this story to strike the men blind, so the Levite thrust his concubine out to the men. She is raped all night while the men sleep inside, and she crawls to the door with her last bit of strength. She is found there by the Levite who simply says, "Get up we are going." She does not answer, so he puts her on one of the animals and goes home. When he gets home, he cuts her into 12 pieces and sends each to one of the 12 tribes. A war is started between the tribes, and the tribe of Benjamin is almost wiped out. The story is every difficult to fathom at all because the crime for which the tribe of Benjamin is presumably punished is the murder of the concubine. Yet, by our way of thinking, the true scoundrel is the Levite who shows zero compassion for his wife.

The story is about brutal, violent, deadly rape and murder which has nothing to do with gender. The men were going to rape someone regardless of sex. However, the narrative has often been interpreted like the Sodom narrative as a condemnation of homosexual activity.

The exegetical points are the following:

- ✓ This is bizarre story. It typifies the lawless character of the time of the book of Judges and the very, very misogynist abuse and oppression of women in that culture. The poor, unnamed woman is ignored, raped, abused, left to die, cut into pieces, and the sin of the town is characterized as inhospitality to male visitors.
- ✓ There are some parallels to the story of Sodom and Gomorrah, and neither story has anything to do with consensual homoeroticism.

EXEGETICAL ANALYSIS

Gagnon is front and center with an interpretation that highlights the initial intent of the men of the town as homosexual. He acknowledges that the rest of the story hinges on the rape and murder of the concubine, which causes a massive holy war in Israel. According to Gagnon, the initial attempt to have sex with the Levite is so vile to the old man that he offers his virgin daughter and the Levite's concubine. "Repugnance for male penetration of males must have been a significant factor in twice designating the demand for sexual intercourse with Levite as a *nebala* (NRSV: vile thing) much greater than that involving intercourse with the old man's daughter and the Levite's concubine."[43] To contemporary society the actions of the Levite putting his concubine out of the house to save his own skin is appalling. Similarly, it is pretty extreme even for a society that considered women chattel. Gagnon discusses the nature of the culture's view of the place of women, but he still believes the driving force for the concubine's treatment is the horror of homosexual anal sex. I must be clear about Gagnon's belief that he is considering homosexual anal sex not just homosexual anal rape.

---

43   Gagnon, p. 95.

Olson's conventional commentary on the text mentions the homosexual rape in passing, but his exegesis on the entire text juxtaposes the treatment of women as a trajectory through the book of Judges. It was a time when "in those days there was no king in Israel; all the people did what was right in their own eyes."[44] As the book progresses the treatment of women gets worse and reaches a low point with this narrative. The culture itself regresses as typified by the Levite's company being left in the town square uninvited until the old man arrives. The citizens should have been falling all over themselves to have a Levite spend the night with them. So the narrative is about the degeneration of Israel during the Judges era, and the Levite himself is an example of the worst of society. Olson notes that we do not even know when the concubine died, and the Levite does not even mention his own culpability when telling the story to Israel.[45]

Boswell has little to say about this text other than to point out its similarity to the story of Lot and Sodom. He brushes off this text with "But Jews and Christians have overwhelmingly failed to interpret this story as being about homosexuality, correctly assessing it as a moral about inhospitality, as did the Levite himself, who recounted the incident to the Israelites he called upon to avenge him without any hint of sexual interest (in him) on the part of the men of Gibeah."[46] Alexander discusses the rape of the concubine at Gibeah. Like some other commentators, he emphasizes the parallel nature of the story with the Sodom story. Once again, inhospitality is a major issue or moral failing on the part of the villagers, and the householder's extreme measure of promising both his virgin daughter and the Levite's concubine speaks volumes of the importance of defending the Levite.[47] Our contemporary society cannot begin to grasp this bizarre defense of hospitality because we have a very different view of women.

---

44   Judges 21:25.
45   Olson, pp. 872-879.
46   Boswell, pp. 95-96.
47   Alexander, pp. 35-36.

Powell dismisses both the Sodom and Levite stories as having nothing to do with homosexuality as we understand it today: "The stories speak only of the sin of homosexual rape and say nothing at all about consensual relations between persons of the same sex.[48] Rogers sort of lumps the two narratives (Sodom with the Levite's concubine) together in talking about the status of women in that ancient culture. In both cases, the host would sacrifice women to the evil crowd to protect the more important men involved. In that culture, to be treated as woman sexually was absolutely humiliating, and a violent rape even worse. Gender issues rather than sexual issues are involved in both stories.[49]

This story is a reflection of the Sodom and Lot story in Genesis. They are set within very different historical contexts: The destruction of Sodom is set in the patriarchal era and contrasts the over-the-top hospitality of Abraham, and the slightly less hospitable Lot, against the extreme hostility of the men of Sodom. While most people remember the intent for the male-male rape of the visitors, especially due to the travesty of word sodomy being applied to male-male anal sex, the story of Sodom is about hospitality, violence, and abuse. Unfortunately, it is also about the position of women at the bottom of the societal ladder. A literal reading of this story would lead one to undervalue (an understatement) women. It would be difficult to preach without turning the story on its head. The greatest "sin" could have been Lot offering his daughters to the crowd!

The story of the Levite's Concubine is even more difficult. The Levite has no redeeming qualities. Both he and the father of the concubine ignore the wishes of the woman who has no words to say on her behalf. The Levite throws his wife to the wolves, opens the door when he is ready to leave, puts her "body" on the animal without even checking to see how she is, and then cuts her up into pieces! On top of that, he tells the Israelites how bad the men of Gibeah are, and starts an intertribal war.

---

48   Childs, *Faithful Conversations*, p. 23.
49   Rogers, pp. 67-68.

It would be hard to get a message about homosexuality out of either of these passages.

THE HOLINESS CODE IN LEVITICUS

5) Leviticus 18:22 *You shall not lie with a male as with a woman; it is an abomination.*

6) Leviticus 20:13 *If a man lies with a male as with a woman, both of them have committed an abomination; they shall be put to death; their blood is upon them.*

These verses are often quoted as a divine command against homosexuality. If two men have sex together as if one were a woman, they are even condemned to death. The consensus opinion is that this "law" declares homoerotic activity a sin today as it supposedly did then. These are commands as opposed to the narrative style found in the earlier scriptures discussed. So they are generally taken literally as written, out of the Levitical context.

Chapters 17-26 in Leviticus are known by many as the Holiness Code because of the repetitive phrase "You shall be holy, for I the Lord your God am holy" (19:2b), but holiness means something different to us than it did this ancient culture. Unlike the early part of Leviticus that is directed to priestly things such as sacrifices, the Holiness Code is directed at the corporate body of Israel. The Israelites were God's chosen and set-aside people. Disappointed with the sinful nature of the people in the world, God chose Abraham to begin the procreation of a people who would be God's own special people. God led the Moses people out of Egypt, much to the chagrin of Pharaoh and his people, and led them to the promised land while displacing the Canaanites who were already in the land.

In order to remain the people of God, God expects them to manifest certain behaviors and attitudes; that is, to be holy. This series of laws was particularly important if much of it was developed during the exile in Babylon. It would have been very easy for the people of Israel to lose their perceived uniqueness and identity and become assimilated into the Babylonian culture and religion. The center of their government, religion, culture, and very existence as a people was the temple in Jerusalem, destroyed in 586 BCE, and the upper crust of society was carried off into Babylon. Judah, the southern kingdom left over from the split of the Davidic kingdom, had not only lost their homeland but also their identity with the loss of the temple. One of the things that helped them survive their captivity as a people was the Holiness Code, because it gave them a uniform way of life that was very different from their captors.

God gave them special treatment and there were requirements of the Israelite culture to maintain their covenantal position. In scripture, many of the forbidden taboos and some positive actions were commanded to set them apart from the Gentile cultures around them—eating certain foods and avoiding other foods, circumcision, wearing hair and beards a certain way—proscriptions that set the people apart. We can call these purity issues, cultic taboos, or cultural issues.

The exegetical points are the following:

- ✓ "You shall not lie with a male as with a woman" is not what the Hebrew says. It is an interpretation of the literal "with a male, you shall not lie down the lyings-down of a woman/wife." There are multiple interpretations of this Hebrew text, and most add "as with a woman" or "like a woman," but the words are not there in the Hebrew.
- ✓ The word that is generally translated as "abomination" (*toevah*) is used for many other admonitions that we consider cultic rather than moral. Eating pork is one of those. There is a lot of argument about this aspect of the text.
- ✓ There is no reference to female-female sexual activity. If same-sex eroticism is morally wrong, why would the author(s) have left out any lesbian concerns? One very possible reason is the intent behind the admonition. The admonition (as unclear as it is) presupposes the high

patriarchal view of men as vastly superior to women. To behave as a woman was exceedingly demeaning on the part of the passive partner and a waste of semen for procreation on the part of the active partner.

✓ In an Israelite view of cosmic order described in creation, many things are "out of order": shrimp should not be eaten because they do not have fins, two cloths should not be mixed in the same garments, and men do not have sex with each other.

✓ The reason for the admonition could be the loss of procreation (waste of semen). If that is the case, it is purely contextual to a time when the continuance of the tribe was crucial, unlike today when over-population is the issue. Also, the emphasis on procreation would argue against celibacy, couples having sex after the age of fertility, and birth control of any kind.

✓ Although breaking this admonition is punished by death, so is the son who curses his parents. Breaking many of these Levitical admonitions is punished by being "cut off" from the people, a punishment that would result in shameful death in exile.

✓ In short, this admonition is not about a moral issue regarding same-sex eroticism.

EXEGETICAL ANALYSIS

Gagnon's analysis of these two scriptures is rather extensive. Leviticus 18:22 appears in a long discourse on various forbidden sexual activities including incest, adultery, child sacrifice, bestiality, and sexual intercourse with a woman who is " in her menstrual uncleanness." Since contemporary society accepts these other admonitions, Gagnon asserts, we should accept the one about male-male sex.

I think Gagnon is saying we are supposed to follow the entire Holiness Code. That would be very interesting, indeed. Adultery in Leviticus means that a man has violated patriarchal laws regarding another man's ownership of his wife, while modern Christians place greater moral admonition on adultery because it breaks a covenant relationship and totally ignore menstrual "uncleanness." Likewise, the detailed Levitical admonitions on incest all relate to patriarchal laws.

Some have argued that the prohibition of male-male sex is only because of the loss of procreation. Gagnon concedes that there are many reasons to assume this possibility, and it juxtaposes well with the Genesis 1 creation command to be fruitful and multiply. However, there are other sexual acts that do not limit procreation that are proscribed, such as the very detailed incest laws. So Gagnon discounts procreation as the central logic behind the law against homoerotic behavior. Gagnon's logic is flawed on this point. The incest laws also have everything to do with procreation, because incest abrogates the clear lines of heritage and inheritance.

Incest prohibitions had nothing to do with inbreeding and genetic abnormalities. People did not have the science to understand that. Since these incest commands only concern the actions of men and not women, they are patriarchal laws. Incest abrogates a man's property rights and can confuse the all-important lineage and inheritance. If a child is born from incest or adultery, to whom does the child belong and what are his inheritance rights? Similarly, we do not know the reason for the precluding of men lying with men as a woman, but this admonition may well have had to do with patriarchal culture. It would certainly be a violation of an androcentric patriarchy for a man to take on a woman's role in intercourse. Why does it matter what reasoning lies behind the admonition? It matters a great deal. If the reasoning (context) has changed from 2500 years ago, then the interpretation might be quite different in a different context. For example; in Deuteronomy 21:18-21, a rebellious son is to be stoned to death at the city gate. The context is one of the crucial elements of preserving family at all costs. Also, the parents (especially the father) are part of the patriarchal structure. Today, we do not have city gates, and we understand family and community life differently.

Gagnon does not accept any distinction between moral and cultic differences when the word *toevah* (translated as abomination) is applied. His warrants are the many times that *toevah* is applied in the rest of the Hebrew scriptures, when it refers to moral and not simply cultic issues. He compiles a laundry list of "abominations" from other Hebrew scripture: murder, swearing falsely, habitual lying, not aiding the poor, robbery, extortion, charging interest, treating parents with contempt, hypocritical prayer of the wicked, marriage to a person who worships different god, and so forth. However, Gagnon is not quite correct. Deuteronomy 14:3 ("Do not eat any detestable thing.") is sometimes mentioned as an example of a purely cultic or boundary issue similar to male-male sex. Gagnon claims that non-Kosher food (pork, shrimp, crawfish, etc.) is defined as only being "detestable" rather than an abomination. In truth, the word used is *toevah*, but the NRSV translates it as detestable rather than an abomination.

Toevah ("abomination" in the NRSV translation) is very strong language. Although *toevah* is used to describe many actions unrelated to male-male sex, male-male sex is the only action that gets its own *toevah* applied. Gagnon's supposition is that the male-male sex is the only time in Leviticus that a single action is referred to with its very own *toevah*.

This particular argument of Gagnon's collapses under the weight of the widespread use of *toevah* to describe things that we would consider part of an ancient cultic disposition. Deuteronomy 17:1 declares that a blemished sacrifice is a *toevah*, and 22:5 makes the same pronouncement against men who wear women's clothes and women who wear men's clothes. In summary, the word *toevah* or abomination that was used by the author(s) expresses a strong admonition against a particular act, but the same word is applied to non-moral issues.

The word *toevah* is applied after lists of actions that we conclude are not relevant anymore or are certainly not worthy of death.

If these two admonitions existed alone and separate from their literary context, they could be interpreted as Gagnon (among other traditionalists) does. But the scriptures do not exist outside of their context. The people of Israel were set apart to be very different from other peoples and nations. Other nations worshipped multiple gods and what we call idols. There were numerous fertility cults and religions involving sex. The Holiness Code was written to provide a mechanism for setting the people of Israel apart for the One God. From this ancient document and culture that precedes the document by many years, it is difficult for us to sort out the differences between cultic (purity/cultural) laws and moral laws. This sorting out is made more difficult by the lack of explanation or reasoning given for each command.

Some folks have argued that the word *toevah* (abomination) applies to cultic or purity prohibitions rather than ethical or moral ones. The constant reference to things that are "unclean" in the Hebrew scriptures, for example, we would consider cultic; that is, those things that set the people of God apart but are not what we would consider moral issues, such as how men should wear their hair. The distinction is difficult for us to fully grasp.

On the other hand, Boswell's main focus is the word *toevah* as it is used to describe men who "lie with a male as with a woman." He draws a complete distinction between something that is a moral issue and that is a ritually unclean. According to him, *toevah* categorically is used to describe something that is ritually unclean rather than immoral. Whether that distinction is iron clad, the context, he argues, is one of ritual purity that sets boundaries for the Israelites as the special or chosen people of God. The beginning of the section (Leviticus 18:3) is a strong admonition to not follow the practices of where the people came from (Egypt) or the people of the land they inherited (Canaan). The Greek translation of the Hebrew scriptures, the Septuagint, even translates *toevah* differently whether it is referring to ritual or moral issues. He is convinced and proves that the early, patristic church did not consider this ritualistic law as binding; just as dietary laws were no longer binding. However, that is not the issue. The issue is what was intended by the writers of Leviticus and what did their readers or listeners understand? It is very difficult for us to draw a solid line between purity and moral issues... if there is such a line to be had.

The penalty (death) is extreme. According to Gagnon, since the death penalty is the commanded punishment for male-male sex in chapter 20, it must be a very serious crime and/or sin against God. Indeed, it does say the death penalty is called for, but the death penalty is also applied to a son who disrespects his parents. Although the death penalty is demanded for male-male sex in Leviticus 20:13, it is also demanded for cursing one's parents, adultery, incest, and bestiality. Yet, to our contemporary society, these are all very different. We cannot imagine the death penalty for back talk from a teenager, even though we may be outraged at the time. In biblical interpretation, taking something out of the biblical context and depositing it in our contemporary context is poor exegesis. One must look at the entire cultural and historical context in which a text appears.

The Israelite culture and religious practices were very different than ours. Their culture was built around an extended family that was very, very patriarchal. The oldest male—father, grandfather, or whatever—was like a king over the rest of the group. The entire operation was based on everybody performing their assigned roles, and there was no other safety net. The family's survival depended on everyone's participation. A son who did not do exactly as he was told with an obedient "yes, sir!" could destroy the family. Adultery, which we Christians believe is sinful because it is a betrayal of covenant, was based on the same patriarchal system. To have sex with a man's wife was a violation of the husband's property rights for which he paid a dowry, and it could interfere with inheritance rights. That is, if a son was born, to whom did he belong? Sons were due an inheritance.

So why was the death penalty prescribed for male-male intercourse? Arguments have been made that male homoeroticism was proscribed because of the "mixing" that is denounced that includes different foods, different cloths, and different crops in the same field. Helminiak asserts that anal sex was a violation of roles, a mixing of kinds, similar to the prohibited mixing of two threads within the same garment or planting two types of seeds in the same field; hence, the mixing of semen with excrement is proscribed. But this argument is weak because the mixing of plant seeds and cloth were not punishable by death.

One of the overarching themes of Genesis, starting with creation, is "order," not "mixing" per se. Mixing is a subset of order. One does not step out of order by eating shrimp because shrimp "don't" belong; they are supposed to have fins like the orderly fish, which is okay to eat. Mixing seeds, animals, cloths, etc., is a lack of order. The boundary being broken by male-male sex is in conflict with the way things are ordered in the creation and by the Mosaic Law in the Holiness Code of Leviticus and the law in Deuteronomy, says Gagnon. But modern Christians do not accept this strict order of the world around us and should not accept "order" that precludes homoeroticism.

It should be no surprise that Gagnon agrees with those who view the logic behind the prohibition as gender-boundary violation based on genital complementarity. He continues to hearken back to the creation myths in Genesis where God established or created, according to Gagnon, the male penis and female vagina. Gagnon argues that the "mixing" that takes place is the non-complementarity or fittedness that he postulates in his discourse on creation. Homoeroticism is a violation of a gender boundary, he says, and again Gagnon's logic is flawed.

Others have argued that the main logic is not physical complementarity that drives the prohibition but the strong patriarchal society; that is, for a man to have sex with another man is to take on the role of woman, which is demeaning for a man. Gagnon's argument against this role violation is that in some scripture the woman does assume a higher role, as in the story of Deborah in Judges 4. However, Gagnon's argument against a misogynist society is weak. Throughout scripture, it is obvious that men wrote everything and considered themselves superior to women. The very society reeked of misogyny as women were pushed to the very bottom of the socio-economic ladder. Yet Gagnon continues to fall back on physical complementarity. The created order includes penises and vaginas, they fit, and that is a moral issue according to Gagnon.

The two scriptures are absolute, he says, and there is no room for exceptions; since both Levitical texts refer to male-male sex, they encompass all of male-male sex. The admonitions are not specific to only certain acts, such as homosexual rape, pederasty, temple/cultic prostitution, Gagnon asserts, so all male-male sex is sinful, whether adult male and young boy, temple prostitutes, or consenting adults.

But Gagnon ignores the context and the implications. When teaching about heteroeroticism, the scriptures make exceptions for the woman who is raped. She is not punished. Yet, there are no specific exemptions given for homosexual rape. There is something missing from the context that we are not privy to. It could be that the context is, indeed, related to idolatry and male temple prostitutes that were common among other nations in that historical era. We really do not know for sure.

One big difficulty that all noninclusionist interpreters, including Gagnon, have is that the Levitical writer did not say anything about lesbian sex. If homoeroticism is a moral issue, then a good question is why does the writer only mention men? The all-important context includes extreme patriarchy. Perhaps a valid comparison is the extremism in some parts of the Middle East that precludes rights for women today. Males were superior to females in every possible way, and wives were simply chattel in society. Male, gay sex degraded one of the men to the female role, which was, indeed, an abomination then. And the other man caused that degradation to occur. In that culture, men were much better and more important than women. Women provided the proper receptacle for carrying the seed given to them. Male, gay sex provided no offspring, which was crucial for the family development and survival. It was a waste of sperm!

Gagnon discusses several reasons why he thinks lesbian activity is not proscribed: 1) lesbianism might have been unknown; 2) in a male-dominated society, such relationships would be impossible; and 3) there was no danger to family structures from female-female eroticism. According to Gagnon, since Jesus introduced interior lust as sinful, lesbian sex should be included in the condemnation of homoeroticism. However, if only interior lust (as Gagnon describes it) were important, Gagnon's whole argument is invalid: all sexual activity would be sinful. Gagnon does not really have an answer to the absence of prohibition against lesbian activity.

Gagnon's responses to those who favor full inclusion of the LGBT community are very instructive. His book represents the most detailed of the technical arguments for excluding LGBT sexual activity from full acceptance.

Verse 18:21, immediately preceding the prohibition of "lying with a male" in 18:22, prohibits child sacrifice to the Canaanite deity Molech. Some have argued that these two verses are related because they specifically prohibit the religious practices of the Canaanites who were dispossessed from the land when Joshua led the people into the promised land. Along with child sacrifice, the Canaanites also practiced homosexual temple prostitution. If the writer had Canaanite practices in mind when writing these verses, then it is possible that the prohibition refers to homosexual temple prostitution that existed among the Canaanites. However, Gagnon argues, that is not true in 20:13, which is embedded among several sexual prohibitions such as incest and bestiality: "... to ban homosexual cult prostitutes was to ban all homosexual intercourse."[50] If the biblical writer(s) had meant to narrow the prohibition to only homosexual prostitution, he says, they could have used the language of Deuteronomy 23:17-18, which specifically identifies female and male prostitution.

These points are all arguable. Allegedly, male prostitutes are forbidden in Deuteronomy, but what is a male prostitute? He could be servicing women as a prostitute. We would all agree that pros-

---

50   Gagnon, p, 131.

titution is immoral whether it is homosexual or heterosexual. We really do not know that context of either text in Leviticus.

Another difficulty that Gagnon and traditionalists have is that many very important people (men, of course) in the scriptures violate the Levitical laws on sex and marriage. For instance, Jacob married two sisters, which is forbidden in Leviticus 18:18. Our contemporary culture has a moral issue with polygamy; we believe it violates the monogamous marriage covenant ordained by God. Yet, the patriarchs, Kings David and Solomon and others, practiced polygamy as if it was the norm. Hence, it is not good exegesis to lift these two texts out of context and apply them directly to our contemporary religious beliefs and faith.

One of the questions that contemporary Christians might have is if we are bound by a law from the book of Leviticus. Gagnon affirms that we are because the apostle Paul makes a similar argument against homoerotic behavior in Romans 1:26-33 (discussed in the section on that scripture).

Conventional commentary, such as that of Kaiser in the *New Interpreters Bible*, takes a conventional view. Kaiser discusses several mitigating circumstances that could allow for homoerotic behavior: 1) the text refers only to sexual activity that is exploitive, violent, lustful, or connected with pagan cults; 2) it is only ceremonial law; and 3) it reflects limited Israelite understandings and social context similar to attitudes on women and slaves that are not germane today. These are reasons that others have suggested. However, even though it arouses some serious emotions on either side of the issue, it says what it says, Kaiser asserts: "The Holiness Code does not consider homosexual activity between men (women are not considered) acceptable and judges it an abomination."[51] Kaiser represents the overall consensus of the traditional view.

Hays offers a short discourse on the Holiness Code scriptures in Leviticus. He flatly states: "This unambiguous legal prohibition stands as the foundation for the subsequent universal rejection

---

51   Kaiser, p. 1127.

of male same-sex intercourse within Judaism."[52] Although he acknowledges that some prohibitions in Leviticus have been eliminated by the early church, he does not agree with the interpreted separation of "purity laws" from "moral laws." The Old Testament makes no such distinction, according to Hays. However, he does concede that some of the Holiness Code is not applicable, so he also turns to the First Testament to determine the moral position on homoerotic activity.

Alter[53] asserts that both scriptures in Leviticus explicitly ban homosexual anal intercourse and intercrural intercourse. According to Alter: "The evident rationale for the prohibition is the wasting of seed in what the law appears to envisage as a kind of grotesque parody of heterosexual intercourse."[54] In brief summary of Alter, homosexual intercourse is proscribed because it is the wasting of male seed. The culture likes to keep lines of categorical distinction clear; yet, although lesbianism was known in the ancient Near East, it is not mentioned at all in either scripture. Why homoerotic behavior was banned is important, although difficult, to understand. If Alter is correct, and I think he is, it is important to know because it helps us to understand whether male-male sex is a moral issue, a purity issue (as in Boswell), or a purely cultural or contextual issue. If it was not a moral issue to the writer, or an issue that is not applicable today, then it is not germane to our own religious/ moral context. For example, we do not mind mixing polyester with cotton, which is expressly prohibited in the Holiness Code. Most people in the American culture today do not regard sexual intercourse as existing only to produce babies. It is a gift from God to be enjoyed. Sperm is wasted in a nocturnal emission, contraception, oral sex, coitus interruptus, and in couples past the age of procreation. It is okay to waste sperm!

Furnish is on the side of moderation in his exegesis of the Hebrew scriptures that are claimed to prohibit male-male homoerotic

---

52   Hays, p. 381.
53   Alter, pp. 623-4.
54   Alter, p. 623.

behavior. In this case, he concedes the literal meaning of the text: "There is no question that the Levitical rule in 18:22 and 20:13 explicitly and unequivocally condemns male same-sex intercourse."[55] However, he questions the reasons behind the prohibition:

- ✓ The intent of the Holiness Code is to identify what is necessary for the people of Israel to remain set apart as God's own chosen people. The rules and commandments are boundary markers. Most especially they prohibit those actions that pollute and defile because they mix kinds that God created as separate, such things as mixing threads or crops in a field. Male same-sex intercourse is an example of violating ritual purity rather than moral purity. Furnish does not recognize any gray area: ritual and moral are distinctly separate, he says. I wish that were true, but I think that the distinction is more nuanced.

- ✓ The word for abomination refers to a "taboo" or a boundary marker. Rather than being a process of moral reasoning, the taboo is rooted in long-standing cultural convention. Moral reasoning is totally absent. For example, there is no exception for homosexual rape. Both the raper and the rapee would be put to death. This is an excellent point that Furnish makes. There are long passages on heterosexual rape and alleged rape, but nothing of the kind for homosexual rape. If a man is raped, should he be put to death?

- ✓ The wording "lying with a man as with a woman" illustrates the patriarchal orientation of this society. Both participants are dishonored, the passive participant for behaving as a woman and the active participant for dominating another male. Distinctive sexual roles are

---

55　Furnish, p. 60.

abrogated. There is no question that Furnish is correct about the patriarchal aspect of that culture.

According to Helminiak, male-male intercourse was not a moral issue but a purity/cultic issue. He lists many other taboos (adultery, incest, and bestiality) that are mentioned in the Holiness Code and also appear elsewhere in scripture, and notes that male-male intercourse does not. Helminiak is splitting hairs between purity issues and moral issues because some of the things mentioned in the Holiness Code are powerful moral issues to us: cheating in business, allowance for gleaning in the fields, prostitution, and the like. He is correct in that these are the only two texts in the Hebrew scriptures that seem to condemn homosexuality explicitly.

Helminiak's calls for the recognition of the distinction between religious taboos versus moral sin. He is very convincing that the abomination of homogenital sex was a taboo and not a moral issue of the culture. It was unacceptable because of taboo or purity laws rather than moral commandment. He does have a point, but it is difficult for us to unravel the intertwining of purity concerns from moral commandments in the Leviticus; we are too far removed from the culture and religious beliefs.

Helminiak's thesis is that the word *toevah*, is purity or cultic violation or taboo rather than a morality based sin. The Hebrew word for an injustice or a sin would be *zimah*. As did Boswell, Helminiak describes the translations in the Septuagint for *toevah*. In 18:22, the Greek translation is *bdelygma* (a detestable thing especially associated with idolatry or other sacrilegious object or event), which is the most commonly used Greek word for *toevah*. Although the Hebrew word *toevah* is used in many places in the Hebrew scriptures, the Septuagint translators used various Greek words to translate it based on their understanding of what was intended by their predecessors. In Proverbs 6:16 and 16:5, *toevah* is translated as *akatharsia* or impure motive. In chapter 16 of Ezekiel, where the author describes the sins of Sodom (not homosexuality, but idolatry, child sacrifice, adultery and basic wickedness), the word used is *anomia* or lawlessness. Ditto for Ezekiel 18:12, 13, and 24, where the discussion is about morality. (It is interesting that Paul used the Septuagint as his reference.)

The English word "abomination" or "abominable" sets our teeth on edge. Something that is an abomination has got to be pretty disgusting to us and, apparently, to God. According to Helminiak,[56] the word is best explained from the following scripture from Leviticus 20:25-26:

> *You shall therefore make a distinction between the clean animal and the unclean, and between the unclean bird and the clean; you shall not bring abomination on yourselves by animal or by bird or by anything with which the ground teems, which I have set apart for you to hold unclean. You shall be holy to me; for I the LORD am holy, and I have separated you from the other peoples to be mine.*

The above text is a very good example of what the Holiness Code is all about. To be set aside or holy requires following certain guidelines that differentiate between the chosen people and surrounding Gentiles. However, Helminiak's argument regarding "abomination" suffers because the Hebrew word here that is translated as abomination is not *toevah* but *shaqats*. He does illuminate the various things that are considered unclean in Leviticus and elsewhere in the five books of law:[57]

- ✓ Dietary laws that eliminate pigs, camels, lobster, and shrimp;
- ✓ weaving cloth from two kinds of thread, or plant two kinds of seeds in the same field (Leviticus 19:19, Deuteronomy 22:11);
- ✓ menstruation in women (Leviticus 15:19);
- ✓ nocturnal emission in a man (Leviticus 15:16, Deuteronomy 23:11);

---

56 Helminiak, p. 56.
57 Helminiak, pp. 57-58.

✓   attending to a burial (Numbers 19:11);

✓   giving birth (Leviticus 12:2-5).

None of these are referred to directly as a *toevah*, so Helminiak's thesis is diluted. However, he makes a comment about the items in the Holiness Code in general that is worth considering: "The ancient Israelites had their own conception about how things should be. They believed that certain rules of consistency of perfection governed God's creation. Fish should have fins and scales (Leviticus 11:9-12, Deuteronomy 14:3-8), so lobsters and shrimp are peculiar."[58] He applies this "God's creation" consistency to other unclean items like pigs and so forth. In a like manner: "In the ancient Hebrew mind, penetrative sex with another man disrupted the ideal order of things and thus was unclean, taboo, forbidden; it was an abomination."[59] He has a good argument.

Countryman is a proponent of full fellowship with the LGBT community, and he takes a different tack from others. His book entitled *Dirt, Greed, & Sex* takes a broader approach than most, speaking to sexual ethics in general rather than the more narrow homosexual ethics. I like this approach because—considering the prevalence of rapes, unwanted pregnancies, AIDS and other STDs, divorces, abusive relationships, slavery, and other sex-related issues—a total approach to human sexuality is needed. The title tells his typology: much of what can be said about sexual morals in scripture can be related to purity (dirt) and property (greed). Others, such as Boswell and Furnish, try to separate moral issues from cultural taboos (purity issues, boundaries, etc.), but, according to Countryman, we are not able to take something written that long ago and decide which "rules" are merely cultural and which are religious. To the writer and Israelites, all of the directives in the Holiness Code (and the Priestly Code) cannot be parsed; they were all to be followed. Eating a little bit of pork was as wrong as adultery because it polluted the land. Concurrently, once he establishes the purity and property foundations of the Holiness Code,

---

58   Helminiak p. 57.
59   Helminiak, p. 58.

Countryman applies that typology to the New Testament, which (in his thinking) "brackets" the old moral codes.

Purity laws are universal though they vary greatly from culture to culture in specifics and importance, but, Countryman says, all "rules relate to boundaries of the human body, especially to its orifices. Whatever passes these boundaries can figure as part of purity law: foods, waste products, shed blood, menstrual blood, sexual emissions, sexual acts, birth, death."[60] The two codes, the Priestly Code (Leviticus Chapters 11-16) and the Holiness Code (Leviticus Chapters 17-26), contain many purity issues:[61]

- ✓ Clean and unclean animals (Chapter 11);
- ✓ a woman's impurity after giving birth (12);
- ✓ leprosy of persons, houses, and textiles or skins (13-14);
- ✓ genital discharges including menstruation (15);
- ✓ slaughter of animals and disposal of blood (17);
- ✓ incest and prohibited sexual acts (18);
- ✓ idolatry, errors in consuming sacrifices, oppression, injustice, hatred, mixture of "kinds," the "foreskin" of fruit trees, blood, haircuts, etc. (19);
- ✓ sacrifice of "seed," wizardry, adultery, incest, and other sexual acts (20);
- ✓ defilement of priests and of their family members, suitability of sacrificial animals (21-22);
- ✓ the festival calendar (23);
- ✓ obligations of resident aliens to observe Torah (24);
- ✓ Sabbath years and jubilees (25);
- ✓ idolatry and Sabbath, blessings and curses regarding keeping of the laws (26).

While the context of purity looms large in Leviticus and other First Testament texts, we are only interested in sexual purity, and more specifically homosexual purity or lack thereof. Sexual acts between males, specifically anal intercourse, was a purity issue

---

60   Countryman, p. 11.
61   Countryman, p. 21.

because both it and cross-dressing "confuse the purer male with the more unclean female."[62] Many commentators believe that the homosexuality is prohibited because it is non-procreative sex, but Countryman does not agree. The issue is purity and property (to be taken up shortly). Since antiquity, Torah interpreters have tried to develop a rationale for the purity regulations. One example is that pork was not healthy; however, there is no evidence of that belief. Countryman quotes Mary Douglas' thesis that much of purity has to do with each individual being a complete specimen of its kind and mixing of kinds. If that were the case, two males having sex would involve a male fulfilling the role of a woman, which is a "combination of kinds" and unclean. However, her thesis and other theses are unable to explain every single purity issue within the Holiness Code and the Torah as a whole. Rather than a unifying theory, custom seems to be the foundation.

According to Countryman, the other defining issue for the Priestly and Holiness Codes is property. It is no surprise that the era in which Leviticus was developed and written was extremely patriarchal. The oldest male of the family structure was like a king (my word, not Countryman's), and the entire family was subservient to him. The family unit itself was the defining societal structure, and everyone in the family, including the patriarch, worked to bring honor and avoid shame on the family. The wife existed to provide incubation for the man's "seed" and provide sons to help with the work. She also ran the household, making clothes, preparing meals, caring for the children, and having lots of babies. She was the property of her husband, with no real rights or privileges. This perspective explains much of the two codes; including the sexual directives. The long lists of incest taboos all revolve around the honor younger males show older males by not having sex with their women. Adultery is a property issue. Since a wife belongs to her husband, if another man has sex with her, he is violating the husband's property rights. The wife was not even considered a member of the family; just property. Countryman never states

---

62   Countryman, p. 23.

what this has to do with homoerotic events; perhaps, the penetratee becomes like property to the penetrator.

Neither purity nor property seems to explain the prohibition against homoerotic behavior. If the penetratee becomes like property and/or becomes unclean like a woman, then what wrong has the penetrator done? Yet, both are to be executed. While Countryman's general thesis on purity and property is quite illuminating, it does not accomplish much in explaining the taboo against homoerotic behavior, except to say that it is a purity issue.

Alexander agrees that these two texts in Leviticus do prohibit male-male sexual intercourse, and he posits two reasons for the prohibition. The first is his interpretation of the word "abomination": it means that the prohibition is for cultic reasons rather than moral reasons. His reasoning here is weak. He provides the example that many sexual acts that we view as acceptable are not performed as part of our "cultic" life; that is … in church. So male-male sex or any sex would not be acceptable in our church. For them, male-male sex was precluded in this cultic life, and it had nothing to do with morals. A stronger reason is that the sperm is wasted. In the ancient world it was believed that life was vested in the male sperm, and women only supplied incubation. Since the procreation of children was crucial for survival of the family, if a male wasted his sperm he was wasting the opportunity to produce life. That is why lesbian sex is not even mentioned, because it does not take away from the production of children.[63]

Jack Rogers covers some of the same ground, although his logical argument is very concise in describing holiness:[64]

- ✓ Israel's worship practices had to be different from the indigenous Canaanites. Everything they did had to set them apart.
- ✓ They could not mix with any other people, and so they generalized this concept to include any kind of mixing: different types of seed, two different materials in the same

---

63   Alexander, pp. 36-39.
64   Rogers, pp. 68-69.

garment.
- ✓ Male gender superiority had to be maintained. A child that cursed parents was to be put to death!
- ✓ A homosexual act was punishable by death because a boundary had been crossed when a man took on the role of a woman. Also, the man being penetrated became impure.
- ✓ Lastly, the word *toevah*, translated as "abomination," is used for ritual impurity. Ritual impurity was what set the Israelites apart from the people around them.

One of the more interesting interpretations of this "abomination" is that those who quote it to condemn homosexual acts ignore the rest of the Holiness Code in Leviticus. There are many admonitions and commands regarding holy living that are contained in this ancient literature. It is forbidden to eat the blood of animals, and the Kosher preparation of meat includes the bleeding out of animals rather than killing them swiftly (17:10-14). It is an abomination (18:29) for a man and woman to engage in sex if the woman is menstruating (18:19). Incest is an abomination (18:1-18). It is wrong to interbreed animals (no mules allowed), mix different fibers in a cloth (no polyester/cotton blends), or plant two kinds of seed in a field (19:19). The Sabbath must be kept and parents honored (19:3-4). It is an abomination to eat a sacrifice after the second day it was offered (19:6-7). We are commanded not to round off our hair at the temples or have tattoos (19:26). Witchcraft is not allowed, and witches are to put to death (19:26; 20:27). Cheating in business is not allowed (19:35-36). Anyone who curses his or her father or mother is to be put to death (20:9). Likewise the adulterer and adulteress are both to be put to death (20:10-16). Of course, the eating of "unclean" food is prohibited (20:25-26 with a great deal of detail as to what is clean and unclean in Leviticus 11:1-47).

Now we ignore many of these laws because our culture is so different than it was then; we have a better scientific understanding of how things work and what can be done. Of course, that is my point: the context has changed over the last 2500 years, and we must take all of this seriously but with a great deal of care. We might dismiss the interbreeding of animals and mixing of fibers, but what about the command and punishment for adultery? We pretty much think that adultery is acceptable. Kim Kardashian got pregnant by Kanye West while she was still married to Kris Humphries, and her celebrity status only went up. How many executions would there be if this law was kept today? My point is not that adulterers should be executed but that we cannot extract pieces of the Holiness Code to claim as law while ignoring others. Some people focus on homosexuality to the exclusion of "you shall love your neighbor as yourself" (19:18b) and the special care we should have for aliens in the land (19:10, 19:33-34, 23:22, 24:22). It is much easier to scapegoat a minority group to make us feel superior to others than to read the scripture that impacts most of society.

Throughout this section on the Levitical texts, all of the exegetes accept the standard translations from various English versions of the Bible. They read the following scripture, "You shall not lie with a male as with a woman," as an admonition against male-male eroticism. The very detailed linguistic analysis of Lings leads him to a very different conclusion. As noted earlier, the literal translation of the Levitical texts is "with a male, you shall not lie down the lyings-down of a woman/wife. "[65] He moves through a lot of translations that have been proposed, but none of the adequately mirror the Hebrew. Most translators have added "as with a woman" or "as you would with a woman," but those words are not present in the Hebrew. Lings traces the history of the interpretation of the text that did not become associated directly with male-male eroticism until the middle ages. His analysis is compelling and should be a part of further conversation and study.

Vines has an interesting section that addresses Levitical law's authority for Christians. He concludes that "Christ's death on the cross liberated Christians from all that—what Paul called the 'yoke

---

65   Lings, p. 235.

of slavery'."[66] His analysis is carefully nuanced, and he appropriately defers to the New Testament.

---

66   Vines pp. 78-86.

PART 1B: THE NEW TESTAMENT CLOBBER VERSES

WHAT DID JESUS HAVE TO SAY ABOUT HOMOSEXUALITY?

WHAT DID JESUS HAVE TO SAY ABOUT HETEROSEXUALITY?

Jesus had nothing to say about homosexuality. He did have a few things to say about heterosexuality.

Matthew 5:27 *You have heard that it was said, 'You shall not commit adultery.'* [28] *But I say to you that everyone who looks at a woman with lust has already committed adultery with her in his heart."*

Matthew 5:31 *It was also said, 'Whoever divorces his wife, let him give her a certificate of divorce.'* [32] *But I say to you that anyone who divorces his wife, except on the ground of unchastity, causes her to commit adultery; and whoever marries a divorced woman commits adultery.*

Luke 16:17 *But it is easier for heaven and earth to pass away, than for one stroke of a letter in the law to be dropped.* [18] *Anyone who divorces his wife and marries another commits adultery, and whoever marries a woman divorced from her husband commits adultery.*

Matthew 19:3 *Some Pharisees came to him, and to test him they asked, "Is it lawful for a man to divorce his wife for any cause?"* [4] *He answered, "Have you not read that the one who made them at the beginning 'made them male and female,'* [5] *and said, 'For this reason a man shall leave his father and mother and be joined to his wife, and the two shall become one flesh'?* [6] *So they are no longer two, but one flesh. Therefore what God has joined together, let no one separate."* [7] *They said to him, "Why then did Moses command us to give a certificate of dismissal and to divorce her?"* [8] *He said to them, "It was because you were so hard-hearted that Moses allowed you to divorce your wives, but from the beginning it was not so.* [9] *And I say to you, whoever divorces his wife, except for unchastity, and marries another commits adultery."*

Mark 10:2 *Some Pharisees came, and to test him they asked, "Is it lawful for a man to divorce his wife?"* [3] *He answered them, "What did Moses command you?"* [4] *They said, "Moses allowed a man to write a certificate of dismissal and to divorce her."* [5] *But Jesus said to them, "Because of your hardness of heart he wrote this commandment for you. 6 But from the beginning of creation, 'God made them male and female.'⁷ 'For this reason a man shall leave his father and mother and be joined to his wife, ⁸ and the two shall become one flesh.' So they are no longer two, but one flesh. ⁹ Therefore what God has joined together, let no one separate."¹⁰ Then in the house the disciples asked him again about this matter. ¹¹ He said to them, "Whoever divorces his wife and marries another commits adultery against her; ¹² and if she divorces her husband and marries another, she commits adultery."*

Jesus said nothing about homosexuality. There are at least several possible reasons for this omission: 1) He did not know that homosexuality existed; 2) He assumed that the texts in Leviticus already covered it; 3) homosexuality was not considered a sin by Jesus; 4) heterosexual marriage, divorce, adultery, and sexual behavior are more important to Jesus; 5) from the above statements by Jesus, it appears that he has a contextual issue with the treatment of women in that culture; and 6) Jesus has a short time in which to accomplish and teach a lot. There could be many more reasons, but we can be sure that he was very concerned about the expression of married, heterosexual behavior.

Jesus viewed marriage as a covenant between two people that was ordained and blessed by God even through our creation in the image of God. To be a part of the creative will of God is to remain married. The verses from Matthew 5 are two of the six great antitheses from the Sermon on the Mount, and the first one extends adultery to include the mere thought of adultery. Intent to sin is sin according to this sermon. Of course, adultery is one of the 10 commandments from the Hebrew scriptures, but the contextual intent of that era was one of male ownership of wives. To have sex with another man's wife was an infringement on his ownership rights. It is fascinating that the Markan Jesus speaks as though women could legally get a divorce in his era. In the Jewish culture it would have been difficult for a woman to get a divorce; perhaps Jesus is addressing the disparity between the rights of men versus the rights of women.

I wonder what Jesus would think about the Defense of Marriage Act (DOMA), legislation enacted to protect marriage by refusing to recognize gay marriage. What is interesting is that about 50 percent of heterosexual marriages end in divorce, which is clearly forbidden by Jesus. Perhaps a true DOMA would make divorce illegal? While I am being facetious, it is interesting that we hear so much about gay marriage and essentially nothing about Jesus' blessing and admonitions of heterosexual marriage. It is easier to scapegoat a minority than it is to live by scripture.

THE APOSTLE PAUL ON HOMOSEXUALITY: UNNATURAL INTERCOURSE

7)   Romans 1:26 *For this reason God gave them up to degrading passions. Their women exchanged natural intercourse for unnatural, [27] and in the same way also the men, giving up natural intercourse with women, were consumed with passion for one another. Men committed shameless acts with men and received in their own persons the due penalty for their error. [28] And since they did not see fit to acknowledge God, God gave them up to a debased mind and to things that should not be done. [29] They were filled with every kind of wickedness, evil, covetousness, malice. Full of envy, murder, strife, deceit, craftiness, they are gossips, [30] slanderers, God-haters, insolent, haughty, boastful, inventors of evil, rebellious toward parents, [31] foolish, faithless, heartless, ruthless. [32] They know God's decree, that those who practice such things deserve to die—yet they not only do them but even applaud others who practice them.*

This is probably the perceived clearest reference to homosexuality in the Second Testament. It is the only one in the entire Bible that refers to women in the context of "unnatural intercourse." The fundamentalist consensus opinion is that Paul is referring to male-male and female-female intercourse in very negative terms. While he produces a list of sins including envy, murder, strife, and the like, he seems to put homosexuality as an example of just how low humankind can fall. According to Paul, the fall to depravity began with the worship of idols. When humankind worshipped idols, God "gave them up" to a multitude of degrading passions, and the first one listed is apparently homosexuality. According to the more obvious, literal interpretation, Paul regards homosexuality as an unnatural expression of human sexuality. It is important to exegete the text within the greater context of the letter to the Romans.

Paul is just beginning to build the case that is introduced in a concise passage in Chapter 1, verses 16 and 17: the gospel message levels the playing field of salvation through faith for all people, both Jew and Gentile (Greek). Since it is the gospel that brings salvation to all people, all people must be in need of salvation, and he starts his argument with the Gentiles. In spite of the obvious revelation of God through his creation, the Gentile communities all chose wrongly by worshipping idols. Idolatry is the overarching sin of the Israelites in the Hebrew Bible, and the sinful posture of the Gentile communities that Paul evangelized throughout his ministry. Although the Gentiles do not have the advantage of being part of the chosen people of God, Paul recognizes no excuse for idolatry. The sin of the Gentiles is idolatry, and their choice of idolatry is a sin because they chose idolatry rather than worship of the true God. Because of their choice not to serve him, God gave them up to "degrading passions."

A long ad hoc list of wicked actions and attitudes follows the reference to sexual activities in verses 26 and 27. These are listed by Paul, with and added to the "shameless" sexual acts that have been lifted out of context by biblical interpreters to prove God's judgment on homosexuality. It should be no great surprise that murder is juxtapositioned along with shameless acts; however, the long list includes indwelling sins of envy, slander, boasting, craftiness, and the like. There is no great distinction or gradient of wickedness between verses 26-27 and the list in verses 29-31. Therefore, if we want to condemn homosexuals on the basis of this text, we must condemn those who gossip. All who practice such things deserve to die! What Paul is trying to do is build the case that all people need the gospel. Paul is using the Gentiles as examples of sinners in need of salvation through Christ, and he is rhetorically setting up those Jews who believe the Covenant is adequate. He drops the other shoe with Romans 2:1: "Therefore you have no excuse, whoever you are, when you judge others; for in passing judgment on another you condemn yourself, because you, the judge, are doing the very same things." No one can be saved on the basis of individual righteousness; "all have sinned and fall short of the glory of God" (Romans 3: 23). Redemption comes from Jesus Christ.

The exegetical points are the following:

✓ The contextual, exegetical argument supporting the inclusion of homosexuals in the life of the church is the overarching theme of the letter itself. Chapter 2 follows this text with a condemnation of those who judge others and a leveling of the playing field between Jews and Gentiles. This text could be interpreted to mean exactly the opposite of what is generally assumed. There is a level playing field, all have sinned, only Christ can save, and be cautious about condemning the "others."

✓ In conjunction with the listing of male-male eroticism, there is a long list of other "sins" requiring death as punishment. It is a travesty to lift one activity out of context and use it to condemn LGBT people.

✓ Female-female eroticism is not mentioned. Females committing unnatural intercourse could likely refer to oral sex or even women on top during intercourse. If Paul meant female-female eroticism, he could have said it a number of ways. Female-female eroticism is not immoral, and male-male eroticism is not immoral either.

✓ There has been a lot of argument over what Paul meant by "natural" and "unnatural." Does it mean "sinful" or simply "unusual" or "untypical"? Paul's use of the Greek language is consistent with untypical or unconventional.

✓ The phrases "exchanged" and "giving up" are consistent with the understanding that homoeroticism is by choice. While we do not know why someone is homosexual or heterosexual (it has been argued between genetics and environment), we do know that it is not a choice.. For those who are homosexual by orientation, the only choice they have is to be celibate or not.

✓ There is a trajectory of interpretation of the scriptures that has been and is led by the Holy Spirit. We used to accept slavery, racism and the subjugation and oppression of women as eternal, moral truths. Our discernment of the same scriptures has changed over the years. The perception that homoeroticism is immoral is based on science that is out of date.

EXEGETICAL ANALYSIS

The work that most clearly, concisely, and convincingly supports the traditional consensus that Paul is condemning the moral sin of male-male and female-female homosexual activities is Gagnon's. His exegesis and word studies are very powerful and well done. He not only gives his own analysis of the text and context within the Pauline literature, but he takes to task a number of authors who have supported full inclusion of the LGBT community. His argument is that homosexual activity is a sin according to Paul. Gagnon maintains his overarching reason, which he derives from the creation narratives in Genesis, that the sin of homosexuality boils down to genital complementarity and procreativity:

> Put in crude terms, Paul in effect argues that even pagans who have no access to the book of Leviticus should know that same-sex eroticism is 'contrary to nature' because the primary sex organs fit male to female, not female to female or male to male. Again by fittedness I mean not only the glove-like physical fit of the penis and vagina but also clues to complementarity provided by procreative capacity and the capacity for mutual and pleasurable stimulation. These clues make clear that the anus, the orifice for excreting waste products, nor the mouth, the orifice for taking in food, are complementary orifices for the male member.[67]

---

67   Gagnon, p. 254.

There are always logical problems when a paradigm is pushed too far. Gagnon has pulled Paul's reasoning out of his own mind and applied it to the extreme. If Paul is thinking and saying this about bodily orifices then the following are also immoral: heterosexual anal sex and heterosexual oral sex. Similarly, lesbian sex cannot be considered immoral because it can occur without penetration.

Gagnon is thorough in attempting to discount the various reasons that have been given for exegeting this text as providing allowances for some homoerotic behavior:

Paul thought homoerotic behavior was dirty or violated purity/ cultic prohibitions but was not immoral or sinful.

Gagnon's discounting arguments:

- ☐ The context of verses 29-31 includes many sins, not just homosexuality.
- ☐ All other Jewish texts regard it as sinful
- ☐ Condemnation by Greco-Roman moralists

Counter argument: Indeed, Paul has many ad hoc "sin" lists in his many letters. Why pick on the LGBT community?

Verses 2:1-3:20 condemn those who condemn homoerotic behavior.

Gagnon's discounting argument: Although the extended argument is spreading a wide net to include all "sinners," Jew and Gentile alike, and even though all can only be saved by the Gospel of Christ Jesus, sin is still sin. "For Paul, God's judgment is still coming on those who do the things described in Romans 1:18-32. Paul believes that those who become redeemed in Christ will, and must, no longer live like the people described in 1:18-32; otherwise, they too will perish."[68]

Counter arguments:

- ☐ If Gagnon's interpretation of sin, grace, and law is correct, then all of humankind is doomed.

---

68   Gagnon, p. 281.

□ The message of Romans is that there is now a level playing field (which includes the LGBT community!), and with grace through the Gospel of Jesus Christ we are saved.

The worship of idols is the necessary prerequisite for homosexuality.

Gagnon's discounting argument: Sin began with Adam, not idolatry.

Counter argument: True, Paul is referring to sin in a general sense that began with Adam. However, Paul's context included many Greeks who worshipped idols and practiced male-male sex, whether pederasty or temple prostitution.

Paul is not referring to the creation narrative that defines the roles of males and females.

Gagnon's discounting argument: "As with Jesus, so with Paul: the creation story in Genesis does not leave room for a legitimate expression of same-sex intercourse."[69]

Counter arguments:

□ Jesus refers to the creation story in condemning divorce; he says nothing about same-sex eroticism. Paul does not refer to the creation story; we do not know what his thinking is.

1:26 does not refer to same-sex intercourse but to heterosexual intercourse. In other words, it does not specifically state what "unnatural intercourse" for women means.

Gagnon's discounting arguments:

□ The phrase "and likewise" in verse 27 links the two verses, so they both mean the same thing
□ Gagnon refers to some extrabiblical sources that list lesbian sex as wrong.

---

69 Gagnon, p. 291.

Counter argument: If Paul meant female same-sex intercourse, he could have said so. We do not know for sure what he meant. If anal sex is his target, he could mean heterosexual anal sex or heterosexual oral sex. Gagnon's extrabiblical sources are not relevant.

Hays begins his analysis of homosexuality with a story about an old and dear friend who died of AIDS, so the reader knows that Hays struggles with the love he had for his friend versus his own straightforward interpretation of the biblical texts. His interpretation is that Paul is condemning both male-male and female-female sexual relations. He is basically in agreement with Gagnon (or Gagnon is in agreement with Hays, since Hays' book was written first) that the creation in Genesis 1:27-28 charges humankind to multiply and 2:18-24 describes the culmination of male-female relationship as they become one flesh.

> Thus the complementarity of male and female is given a theological grounding in God's creative activity. By way of sharp contrast, in Romans 1 Paul portrays homosexual behavior as a 'sacrament' (so to speak) of the antireligion of human beings who refuse to honor God as Creator. When human beings engage in homosexual activity, they enact an outward and visible sign of an inward and spiritual reality: the rejection of the Creator's design.[70]

Interestingly, Hays identifies Paul's understanding of nature or natural with the created order. The created "order," as I understand Genesis and Leviticus, is powered by the ancient writers' understanding of order that includes foods, clothing, crops in the field, and much that exists in God's creation. The ancient religious writers and oral precursors understood creation as something of order rather than chaos. Stepping out of order is not a moral issue in contemporary society, but it could entail breaking taboos just as it did in ancient times. Hays does not interpret breaking the established order as a taboo or purity issue, but interprets it as a moral, spiritual, or religious issue.

---

70   Hays, p. 386.

Hays is obviously struggling with his past relationship with his good friend and what he interprets regarding homosexuality: "Homosexual acts are not, however, specially reprehensible sins; they are no worse than any other manifestations of human unrighteousness listed ... no worse in principal than covetousness or gossip ... Homosexual activity will not incur God's punishment: it is its own punishment ..."[71] Based on Romans 2:1, Hays rightly warns those who would condemn homosexual people that self-righteous judgment is just as bad as the homosexual behavior itself. So Hays is not going to give homosexual people a pass, but he is going to defend them against scapegoating! Unfortunately, his solution is impractical and unfair. Like many people, he proposes a life of celibacy for those who would be homosexual. For heterosexual people, the prescription is celibacy or sex within the marriage covenant, but homosexual people cannot marry.

In the *Anchor Bible Dictionary*, Charles Myers points out a few exegetical issues of importance. It is true that homosexual behavior between consenting males was a capital offense in Israel (Leviticus 18:19; 20:18), but so were such heinous crimes as consulting a medium or wizard, cursing your father or mother, and engaging in sexual intercourse with a menstruating woman: "It is vital to note that Paul's presuppositions about homosexuality in Romans 1 are similar to those of his contemporaries. Paul's choice of the active verbs "exchanged" (1:26) and "giving up" (1:27) assume that homosexuality is an activity freely chosen. Paul's use of the phrase "consumed with passion" (1:27) reveals the belief that homosexual behavior is associated with insatiable lust and unbridled passion."[72]

We now know that homosexuality is not a choice but a discovery. Therefore, the context for interpreting this scripture has changed dramatically. Myers' point is very interesting: Paul's wording is "giving up (*aphiemi*) natural intercourse with women ..." which means to freely give up or change. Paul lived in a non-scientific era when it was thought the earth was flat, the sun went

---

71   Hays, p. 388.
72   Myers, pp. 827.

through the heavens from east to west, and homosexual activity was chosen. Today, we know that homosexuality is discovered and not chosen.

Myers notes that in the context of these texts through 2:1 Paul transcends the lists of sins by noting that those who condemn people for practicing these sins are just as guilty: "Therefore you have no excuse, whoever you are, when you judge others; for in passing judgment on another you condemn yourself, because you, the judge, are doing the very same things."[73] Does this mean that those who condemn/oppress homosexuality actually condemn themselves, or that declaring a homosexual person a sinner is a sin?

Due diligence requires the following disclosure: many (if not most) traditional, peer-reviewed, scholarly publications disagree with me; that is, they interpret verses 26 and 27 as referring to homosexual activity regardless of context. Fitzmyer[74] is one of those who interpret this text in the more traditional vein. According to him, homosexuality was quite prevalent in the Greco-Roman world that Paul addressed: "Second, Paul sees homosexual conduct as a symbol of the perversion stemming from idolatry. For him it is a way in which human beings refuse to acknowledge the manifestation of God's activity in creation. The human being who fails to acknowledge God and turns from him, who is the source of life and immortality, seeks rather a vicarious expression of it through the misuse of the natural procreative faculty."[75] Paul perceives that homosexuality is against nature according to Fitzmyer. A crude way of putting this position is that "the parts don't fit and a baby is not produced." Of course, my take on this interpretation is that if God creates homosexuals, how is that creation not natural? I wonder what Fitzmyer's position would be today, some 20 years later? One of the leading Bible scholars of our era, Fitzmyer is currently part of the Jesuit community at Georgetown University, Washington, D.C.

---

73   Romans 2:1.
74   Fitzmyer, pp. 275-276 and pp. 285-288.
75   Fitzmyer, p 276.

Famous and prolific exegete N. T. Wright takes a measured and balanced yet traditional approach to Paul's meaning in this text. Regardless of the many ways of rationalizing or mitigating what Paul says, Wright writes, "it is clear that he regards homosexual practice as a dangerous distortion of God's intention."[76] Being very aware of the contemporary "controversy" or moral/ethical/political arguments regarding homosexual practice, Wright walks a fine line between the two sides of the issue: "It is quite logical to say that we disagree with Paul or that in light of our greater knowledge of human psychology we need to assess the matter ... what we cannot do is to sideline this passage as irrelevant to Christian ethical discourse ...."[77] He notes that Paul's most damaging condemnation is reserved for those who adopt an air of moral virtue.

Everett Kalin,[78] Professor Emeritus of New Testament at Pacific Lutheran Theological Seminary, delves deeply into the overall content and context of the section from Romans 1:18-3:20. The letter is written to Christians, but the section covers first Gentiles and then Jews. While Paul emphasizes the "unnatural" sexual habits of the idol worshippers (Gentiles), he also lists a number of actions and evil attitudes that characterize those that God has given up to degrading passion. Even though they have a special covenant and the Law, Jews have not been saved through the Law. But the core of the message, according to Kalin is verse 2:1: "Therefore you have no excuse, whoever you are, when you judge others; for in passing judgment on another you condemn yourself, because you, the judge, are doing the very same things."

The "therefore" links everything before it back to verse 18, and the great "ungodliness" and "wickedness" is those who judge others as unfit. This focus is very consistent with the message of Romans that salvation only comes through faith and without Christ we are all sinners trapped by the power of sin. Paul's anthropology is quite pessimistic but necessitates salvific faith. Kalin is addressing

---

76   Wright, p. 435.
77   Wright, p. 435.
78   Kalin, pp. 423-432.

clergy ordination, and he interprets the core message as a warning to be careful about excluding homosexual people from ordained ministry. By excluding them, those who do the excluding are falling into the trap of verse 2:1. Is it too great an extrapolation to say that married heterosexual people who judge homosexual couples unfit for marriage also fall into the same trap?

Kalin closes his analysis with two points for those who want to take Paul seriously and yet welcome gay people into pastoral ministry: "(1) trying to determine with specificity what it was these verses were condemning, given the context of the first-century Mediterranean world and (2) showing how a modern understanding of human sexuality, which can speak of a person's "sexual orientation," puts the issue in a whole new context and makes it impossible simply to quote Paul and close the discussion."[79] Amen!

James Miller[80] presents a very convincing argument that verse 26 does not refer to female homosexuality or lesbianism even though verse 27 does refer to male homosexuality. He has done a huge amount of research into the use of various Greek words in non-biblical resources and the characterization of homosexuality in various Greek contexts. The unnatural sexual activity referred to in verse 26 is heterosexual oral or anal sex. If he is correct, and I think he is because others have interpreted this verse similarly, then there is no reference to female same-sex activity in the Bible. My own interpretation of the references in Leviticus (priestly source) to men lying with men has to do with preserving male semen for procreation. Male homosexuality and anal sex with a female both preclude the application of semen for procreation. The lack of female-female prohibitions is very important. If male-male homosexual intercourse is immoral, why is female-female homosexual activity not prohibited? If the reason for the prohibition of male-male sexual intercourse is the waste of semen, then the reason is not really a moral reason. The reasoning is based in an era when procreation for survival of the family unit was necessary.

---

79   Kalin. p. 432.
80   Miller, pp. 1-11.

Mark D. Smith[81] takes on those who claim that Paul refers only to pederasty in this text and in 1 Corinthians. If the only model of homosexuality that Paul is familiar with is pederasty, then he is only condemning pederasty, which we would agree with because of its exploitative nature. However, Smith lists a number of references that refer to other forms of homosexuality in Paul's context. Smith has a point against those who would explain away Romans by saying Paul was only referring to pederasty.

One of the more intensive studies of verses 26 and 27 has been accomplished by Karl Kuhn of Lakeland College in Sheboygan, Wisconsin. He is sympathetic to more contemporary efforts to rescue homosexual activity from the jaws of judgment, but at the same time, he has been consistent with translation, contexts, and the intent of Paul. He discounts some of the more prevalent efforts to rescue the texts. He discounts the belief that Paul is only referring to pederasty because other models of homosexuality existed in the extrabiblical literature. He also discounts explanations that emphasize the sin of the "passion" as opposed to the act itself.

Kuhn incorporates a broad hermeneutic of canonical context, realizing that canon is not a fixed set of laws but is made up of dynamic narrative, in the sense that the canon has a trajectory in the canon itself and after the canon was "closed." The canon is related to the work of the Holy Spirit: "Many Christians hold to the conviction that the Holy Spirit continues to deepen our understanding of God's will in new times and places, through Scripture, prayer, and shared reflection upon our experiences as people of faith."[82] Within the canon there is an obvious trajectory as evidenced profoundly by Jesus' Sermon on the Mount, that dramatically changes some teachings from the Hebrew Scriptures while Jesus claims to fulfill the law rather than change it. There is a trajectory even between the various gospel accounts in the Greek Scriptures. That trajectory continues today: consider the role of women in the church as expressed in scripture. The typical static,

---

81   Smith, pp. 223-256.
82   Kuhn, p. 320.

binding norm retrieved from scripture would look something like the following: "The (still common) interpretation resulting from such deliberation would likely be that, indeed, women can play an active, important role in the church's ministry, as long as they are subordinate to men, silent in worship, do not ask questions of anyone (except their husbands in the quiet and comfort of their own patriarchal homes), and make a lot of babies!"[83] A similar example is given by Kuhn for the argument on slavery from a previous era: "The Spirit has led us to grasp the dehumanizing and dispiriting consequences of slavery and patriarchy and has called us instead to adopt ways of relating to one another that reap blessing rather than cursing."[84]

The answer to getting past this static interpretation is given by a broad treatment of the entire canon. We are called upon by Christ to love one another, our neighbor, and even our enemies. Love and commitment define relationships within this more dynamic canon rather than static norms. As Kuhn says:

> Many individuals and faith communities believe that they are sensing Jesus' persistent voice. It is a voice revealing to them that those living in committed, same-sex relationships may also bear witness to the mutuality, care, respect, and love that is to characterize all of our relationships with one another. It is a voice disclosing that the best of these relationships, like the best of their heterosexual counterparts, proclaim and give glory to the ways of God. Many of our fellow believers disagree. But as others of us do the best we can to "discern the spirits," our strong sense is that it is the one Spirit at work in these relationships to reveal what it means to be the people of God.[85]

Victor Paul Furnish takes a different tack from some apologists who favor full inclusion of the LGBT community. He concedes the literal natures of the scripture that condemns male-male and female-female eroticism. These activities he associates with the "de-

---

83   Kuhn, p. 327.
84   Kuhn, p. 328.
85   Kuhn, p. 329.

grading passions" and "shameless acts" that follow from idolatry. What Furnish does in his chapter on homosexuality is to discern the reasons behind Paul's words. This particular reference to homoeroticism and the other lists of vices that follow shortly are not part of any moral directive and do not stand with the chapters on ethical appeals (Chapters 12-15). The message of these verses is essentially that these are consequences of the fundamental sin of idolatry, and that they are all the penalty of that basic sin. Like others of his era, Paul regarded homoeroticism as a violation of the created order. The word "exchanged" implies that choices were involved rather than discovery, and those choices were driven by degraded desires and uncontrolled lust. The Good News (Gospel) comes after the depiction of humankind, both Greek and Jew, as having the saving grace of God through Christ Jesus… even sinners.

Furnish summarizes Paul's moral theology on homoeroticism:

✓ There are only two short passages in Paul's letters that mention homoeroticism, and neither time is it Paul's subject. Paul's message is not about homoeroticism; it is about the Gospel message that informs our ability to discern sexual and other moral issues.

✓ Context, Context, Context. In Romans the context is the overall moral chaos of humankind that will be rescued via the good news to be presented later in his argument. The Gospel, according to Paul, is that "humankind is the creation of a just, loving, and faithful God, made in God's image as it is revealed in Christ; and that humankind defiantly refusing to honor and give thanks to God, is being redeemed, renewed, and restored by God's unconditional love."[86] The Gospel requires us to challenge our own presuppositions.

---

86   Furnish, p. 91.

✓ Paul was a person of his world, which formed his significant presuppositions:

> » Sex was for propagation of the species;
> » Homoerotic sex was against "nature," violates male superiority, and undermines the political and social order of patriarchy;
> » Homoeroticism was caused by inordinate passions and lust.
> » None of these presuppositions are valid in our contemporary society. The understanding of "orientation" renders the old presuppositions obsolete.

Countryman's typology includes dirt and greed or impurity and property to characterize Paul's writings as he also does for Leviticus. The distinct reference to homoerotic behavior he attributes to impurity issues. Paul avoided the use of several Greek words that could have been used instead of *atimia pathos* (degrading passions) in verse 26 and *aschemosune* (shameless acts) in verse 27. Paul could have used *hamartia* (sin), *anomia* (lawlessness or transgression), *adikia* (unrighteousness), or *asebeia* (impiety). In verse 29, the list of "vices" begins with *adikia* and *poneria*, or unrighteousness and wickedness, both of which are moral or ethical terms familiar to Paul and his audience. According to Countryman (who wrote the Greek textbook that I used in seminary), homoerotic behavior is contrary to Paul's culture, decency, honor, and it is just what does not happen in polite company, but it is not a sin. Paul viewed it as part of the defining culture of the Greeks. If homoerotic behavior is contrary to nature, it is from the Stoic world that Paul draws this vocabulary. The sins listed in verses 29-31 are just plain sins.

Countryman suggests a very different translation and, hence, a unique interpretation of verses 28-32. His interpretation seems like a bit of fantasy at first, but upon reviewing the translation in detail, it makes a lot of sense. Verse 29 starts out "They were filled with every kind of wickedness..." according to the NRSV. Other translations are somewhat similar. However, the word for filled is *pepleromenous*, which is a perfect passive participle, a form that specifically designates a state of being already in existence at the time of the main verb. The main verb in this case is 'surrendered,' and the perfect passive participle *pepleromenous* implies that the people were already guilty of the following list of offenses when God 'surrendered' them to the punishment of same-gender desires and acts."[87] So the long list of real sins went hand-in-hand with idolatry that caught God's attention. He then surrendered them to base desires of homosexuality. God surrendered them "since they were already filled with all unrighteousness ...."[88] Those base desires and homoerotic activities he treated as being unclean, dishonorable, improper, and against nature, but Paul does not use the extensive vocabulary for sin to describe them that he could have.

Among the earliest of the apologists is Boswell. Boswell is very concerned to eliminate contemporary prejudice against the LGBT community using history, tradition, theology, and scripture. Although the condemnations of homosexuality in Romans appear among references to idolatry, Boswell discounts the possibility that Paul is referring only to temple prostitution. There is vocabulary that Paul could have used for making that case. Rather the persons that Paul condemns in the Roman or Gentile culture are manifestly not homosexual: he is referring to heterosexuals who have turned from God to idols and turned from "natural" male-female sex to same-sex erotic acts. We understand the gay orientation, and it is anachronistic to read homosexuality back into Paul's writings.

Contextually, Paul is correct. The Roman or Gentile culture tolerated or even encouraged homoerotic behavior whether it was pederasty, temple orgies, patron and servant, or whatever. Paul is characterizing the nature of the Gentile culture by the excess of lust that has resulted in same-sex eroticism among the general citizenry. Paul uses the same "against nature" or *para physin* in Romans 11:24 to refer to God grafting the Gentiles contrary to nature onto a good

---

87   Countryman, p. 115.
88   Countryman's translation on p. 115.

olive tree with the Jews. Since Paul characterizes God's activity as "against nature," he can hardly be using "against nature" to refer to moral sins. Paul's overarching theme in Romans is that all have sinned, but Christ has leveled the playing field, and all, whether Jew or Gentile, man or woman, slave or free, can be saved through the Gospel of Christ Jesus.

Vines is absolutely convinced that Paul is referring to excess lust or sexual passion. "In Paul's day, same-sex relations were a potent symbol of sexual excess. They offered an effective illustration of Paul's argument: We lose control when we are left to our own devices. We have no moral anchor without God, so chaos and confusion are a typical result when we abandon him."[89]

Helminiak quotes both Countryman and Boswell as his predecessors, and he sounds somewhat like them. He insists that verses 26 and 27 refer to activities that are contrary to culture rather than immoral. 1 Corinthians, which was written by Paul before he wrote Romans, uses the term *physin* to refer to cultural/cultic norms regarding hair: "Does not nature (*physin*) itself teach you that if a man wears long hair, it is degrading to him, but if a woman has long hair, it is her glory? For her hair is given to her for a covering."[90] Long hair was degrading because it was not considered "normal" in a sense of agreeing with what was expected. Remember the hippie era? Long hair was not immoral, but many of us looked askance at long-haired, freaky people. Helminiak argues that "For Paul, the word *natural* does not mean 'in accord with universal laws.' Rather, *natural* refers to what is characteristic, consistent, ordinary, standard, expected and regular."[91] Paul understood nature as the characteristics of a person or culture, not as a philosophical or theological term.

One should wonder why Paul would use homoeroticism as an example of the shame or degradation of Greek culture. Paul is trying to level the playing field between Jewish Christians and Greek

---

89   Vines, p. 124.
90   1 Corinthians 11:14-15.
91   Helminiak, p. 79.

Christians, Jews and Gentiles who are Christian. Rhetorically he is laying a trap for the Jewish Christian readers or listeners by setting up a "straw man" argument that they will buy into. They will intellectually agree with Paul about the shameful culture of the Gentiles and be caught off guard by verse 2:1 that will incriminate them for judging the Gentile. By using this complicated argument, Paul is illustrating that purity/cultural taboos like eating kosher food, circumcision, and homoeroticism are not important. The real sins listed in verses 29-31 matter because all are guilty, all are sinners, and all are saved by the gospel of Christ Jesus.

However, why didn't Paul pick something else besides homoeroticism? Why not circumcision? Or eating pork? The latter was disgusting to the Jew and definitely practiced by the Gentile culture. Both food (idol meat) and circumcision were major controversial arguments among Jewish Christians and between Jewish and Gentile Christians. Homoeroticism was not. Paul's mention of homoeroticism could let the Jewish Christians feel superior, until Paul dropped the hammer on them, without accusing the Gentile Christians of real sin that was any different from the Jewish Christians.

It is hard to follow Helminiak's logic, and it is difficult to consider that Paul is not calling homoeroticism a moral sin. However, it does become clear that he is putting it in a different classification than the laundry list of sins in verses 29-31. The artificial break between Chapters 1 and 2 makes it difficult to see Helminiak's reasoning, but the comparison Paul makes between Gentile and Christian Jews is evidently about verses 29-31. Yes, Jewish culture does not practice homoeroticism and Gentile culture does, but both Jews and Gentiles are guilty of 29-31, and hence, both are saved by Christ, not law(s).

Mark Allan Powell's analysis is quite different from other authors. Paul is rhetorically pointing toward his conclusion that all have sinned and we should not judge others because we are sinners ourselves. We should all become aware of our need for atonement. Powell notes that Paul begins his argument with an example that everyone would agree with: "He seems to mention same-sex intercourse because he wants to start the discussion with what he believes will be an obvious example. He expects his readers to regard "unnatural" sex acts between two women or two men as not only immoral, but disgusting; once he has them hooked into condemning *those* sinners, he intends to move in and discuss some matters closer at hand (starting with 2:1)."[92] It is difficult to know what Paul considers as immoral or not in this case because of the vocabulary that he uses, but the biggest thing that argues against Paul (and his readers) considering homoeroticism as being the example of immorality is the following question: Why does he need the big list in verses 29-31? If the readers are hooked with verses 26-27, why not just go straight to 2:1 and use the long list after 2:1 to remind the Jewish Christians of their own sins?

Powell's next move is to ask what should those people who are engaged in same-sex relationships do instead? The church's traditional response has been two-fold: 1) change from homosexual relationships to heterosexual, or 2) remain celibate. Considering the more modern understanding of sexual orientation, Powell says the first solution is usually not practical. I would add that it is not only impractical but stupid advice. I do personally know of men who have married and had children only to finally come out of the closet, get divorced from their faithful wives, and engage in a homosexual relationship. The impact on everyone is completely devastating, to the ex-wife and children in particular. So that leaves the second option, which says that it is okay to have a homosexual orientation, but one cannot fulfill sexual desires.

However, according to Powell, imposed celibacy is not scriptural either. Powell quotes Matthew 19:11 where Jesus says that celibacy (a eunuch) is something that "not everyone can accept... but only those to whom it is given." Paul likewise states that those who embrace celibacy may burn with passion which is not pleasing to God (1 Corinthians 7:9). So Powell creates a conundrum within the church's teaching: homosexuals must remain celibate, but the

---

92   Childs, *Faithful Conversations*. pp. 27-28.

church also teaches that celibacy is not pleasing to God. My perception is that if we go back to the very beginning of creation, it is clear that God created us with the ability to love, to love Him and to love each other. Relational love that includes sex is a gift from God that most of us want to embrace. Forced celibacy can be very dangerous as evidenced by the preponderance of pedophilia among Roman Catholic priests a few years ago. Powell poignantly and eloquently reminds us that sexual relationships are much more than sex. Fulfillment for many comes with a lifelong partner in which to share many joys and sorrows. Also, Paul's writing says that turning away from God to idols leads to homoeroticism. What about couples who are abiding and faithful Christians? (Are all idol worshippers engaged in homoeroticism? Are all homosexuals idolaters?)

There are no easy answers, but Powell provides some recommendations, including that the church consider recognizing some same-sex relationships. In doing so, the church would be trying to balance the two sides of scripture: 1) that homoeroticism is sinful, and 2) that forced celibacy is not God's will either. Approval of these relationships would have the following characteristics:

- ✓ The policy would not condone homosexual relationships as normative; they would be exceptions.
- ✓ These relationships would not be considered marriages.
- ✓ Relationships would be defined, not specific sex acts. (This is true for marriage, also.)
- ✓ The church would not reject other approaches, such as celibacy or therapy.

I congratulate Powell on having the courage to conjecture on a solution that attempts to accommodate both sides of the argument. Remember, one side of the argument is the traditional one that says homosexual people must remain celibate. The other side says we should recognize homosexual marriages. However, Powell's suggestion will not work:

- ✓ Heterosexual couples can get married even if they are

atheist, incompatible, incorrigible, or only interested in
the wedding and not committed to a lifelong relationship.
The church will sanction and perform the wedding even
if the marriage does not have a chance of lasting. What
sanctioning body would determine whether a particular
homosexual relationship can be approved by the church
or not?

✓ If they are not marriages, what are they? Now that gay
marriage is legal in the United States what will the church
orchestrate that is something less? Gay unions? What do
they represent? Legal status? How about blessings on the
couple? What does that represent?

✓ Reparative therapy is bogus. The church should not even
recognize it as viable.

Alexander discusses the overall message of the Romans and especially the first three chapters, where Paul is focused on convincing
his readers that all are sinners and require redemption. Alexander's
views of verses 26 and 27 are logical. Verse 26 does not necessarily
refer to female-female eroticism. Unnatural sexual acts would be
something that was not the norm. Things that were not the norm
for women were anal sex, coitus interruptus, and the woman taking
the superior position in sex. On the other hand, verse 27 does refer
to male-male sex. Each of Paul's letters was written to address specific questions, issues, problems, and correspondence in, with, and
from the various churches. Paul writing to a church that he did not
plant or ever visit was writing to address concrete situations there
that we are not privy to. Things said within a letter may be obvious to the addressee but hard to fathom to an outsider, and we are
outsiders. Paul is mentioning sexual activity that is related to their
culture and era. Alexander notes that many exegetes interpret Paul
as referring to pederasty, which was very prominent in the Roman
culture. Alexander does not mention it, but some also think Paul
could be referring to temple prostitution, which was also prevalent.

Rogers begins his analysis of Romans with a statement of his thesis: "I believe, however, that a close and careful look at the text, using the best methods of biblical interpretation, will reveal that Paul is making a statement about idolatry, not sexuality, per se, and that Paul's writings also reflect many cultural assumptions of his time …. The Gospel that Paul is proclaiming in Romans does not center on the issue of sexuality. It focuses on the universality of sin and the free grace of salvation through the life, death, and resurrection of Jesus Christ. That is the essence of the Christian message."[93]

For Paul, the terms "natural" and "unnatural" simply mean "conventional" and "unconventional." The most significant evidence of this meaning is found in 11:13-24 where Paul says that God acts in an unconventional way by grafting the Gentiles onto the tree of God's people. God would certainly not act in an immoral way, but in an unusual or unconventional way. Paul does accept that the conventional way of acting is through heterosexual rather than homosexual activity. I note that Gagnon's whole argument is built upon genital fittedness as the natural way given in creation. For the culture of Paul's day and for Paul, the natural way, heterosexual, is a function of gender roles. Homoeroticism violates gender roles as does long hair on men and short hair on women (1 Corinthians 11:14).

Rogers exposes some common myths about homosexuality that have become presuppositions for people who study scripture related to sexuality. One of the biggest presuppositions is that homosexuality is a "lifestyle" that is chosen; therefore, if the person really tried or prayed or had reparative therapy, he or she could be "cured." I find it difficult to believe anyone still thinks this way, but many do. However, those who attempt to "change" homosexuals are actually trying to modify behavior. Rogers notes that sexual orientation is somewhat like "handedness"… some people are left-handed and some are right-handed. My father went to parochial elementary school, and the teachers would rap the knuckles of children writing with their left hands, because writing with the

---

93   Rogers, p. 73.

left hand was wrong. But we are what we are. Rogers says of gay marriage that "The church should celebrate such unions, rather than imposing unbiblical and unscientific assumptions upon this group of people."

So what conclusions can we draw from Paul's writings in Romans?

- ✓ Paul's rhetoric, theology, and Christology are the context in which these two verses are embedded. He is creating a rhetorical trap for the reader/listener, especially the Jewish Christian reader, who will shake his/her head in agreement about the idolatrous Gentiles whose culture is shameful (homosexuality) and sinful (a long list of sins). Then Paul drops the other shoe that "you" are just as sinful! The level playing field between Greek and Jew is good news because the gospel of Jesus Christ can redeem all.

- ✓ Verse 26 has been interpreted as referring to female-female eroticism. This interpretation is faulty. It does not say that. If homoeroticism is scripturally sinful, why is female-female eroticism never mentioned in the Bible... anywhere? If same-sex eroticism is immoral, it would be immoral for either sex.

- ✓ Gagnon's penis/vagina fittedness does not define relationships or love. While heterosexuals may well find homoeroticism extremely distasteful, relationships transcend sexual activity.

- ✓ Paul was a man of his era, and he had presuppositions based on the two cultures in which he lived, his own Pharisaic Jewish culture and the Gentile or Greek culture of the world around him. His lenses of presupposition told him that homoeroticism was shameful, but not sinful. Paul's vocabulary relating to sexual activity does not indicate sin. On the other hand, the list of sins in verses 29-31 are definitely listed as sins.

✓ Paul broke two distinct "qualities" apart. The homoeroticism that he referred to in verse 27 was something that characterized the Gentile culture, and the list of sins in verses 29-31 characterized both Gentile and Jew as sinful.

✓ There are a multitude of possible reasons that Paul might have thought homoeroticism was shameful:

» It does not produce children.

» In a patriarchal society (both were patriarchal) the superiority of men was compromised by anal sex.

» Homoeroticism was thought to be a choice of lifestyle. Paul's wording states that the idolaters were "giving up natural intercourse with women…."

» Homoeroticism was thought to be caused by excess passion.

None of these reasons are viable today.

✓ To Paul, natural and unnatural refer to the characteristics of a culture, thing, or person, not to natural theology or religion that was developed centuries later than Paul. Paul's discourse on the unnatural sex of the Gentile community referred to a characteristic of that culture (as he saw it).

✓ There is the God-given gift of companionship (which includes sex) from God. Homosexuality cannot be "cured," it is not a disease or abnormality. So there is a grossly unfair conundrum in denying people that relationship by insisting on celibacy.

✓ The church has moved to accept divorce and sanctify remarriage, which is clearly abrogated by Jesus. Why should we single out others as scapegoats?

There is no good reason to deny gay marriages based on Romans 1:26-27.

THE APOSTLE PAUL ON HOMOSEXUALITY:
1 CORINTHIANS

8)   1 Corinthians 6:9 *Do you not know that wrongdoers will not inherit the kingdom of God? Do not be deceived! Fornicators, idolaters, adulterers, male prostitutes, sodomites,* [10] *thieves, the greedy, drunkards, revilers, robbers—none of these will inherit the kingdom of God.* [11] *And this is what some of you used to be. But you were washed, you were sanctified, you were justified in the name of the Lord Jesus Christ and in the Spirit of our God.*

This list contains two words (4th and 5th) that have been used to interpret an exclusion of homosexuals from the kingdom of God. The first word in the Greek is *malakos*, which has been translated a number of different ways. In the NRSV, above, and the popular New International Version (NIV), it has been rendered as "male prostitute." The King James Version (KJV) and the American Standard Version (ASV) translate it as "effeminate"; the Revised Standard Version (RSV) lumps *malakos* with the next Greek word (*arsenokoites*) and comes up with "sexual perverts"; and the New Jerusalem Bible (NJB) translates it as "the self-indulgent."[94]

The root word appears also in Matthew 11:8 and Luke 7:25 in reference to Jesus speaking of John the Baptist: "Why then did you go out? To see a man clothed in soft raiment? Behold, those who wear soft raiment are in kings' houses." A *malakos* in this usage by Jesus refers to a person dressed in soft raiment as opposed to the real John the Baptist, who was a sort of rough and tumble kind of person. Obviously, there is no real consensus on the correct translation of *malakos*. If it is intended to be sexual in nature, it could refer to the practice of pederasty among the Greek/Gentile culture. A male of higher socioeconomic standing would have a boy (often a slave) to mentor and use as a sexual partner. The "person dressed in soft raiment" could refer to the boy prostitute or catamite in the relationship. We would heartily denounce such a relationship today just as Paul did. Male and female prostitutes functioned in

---

94   http://www.religioustolerance.org/hom_bibc1.htm#

some of the pagan religious temples of the Greco-Roman culture. We also would declare male prostitution sinful whether it was a boy or an adult.

The second word, immediately after *malakos*, is *arsenokoites*, which is a word that Paul uses here and appears also in 1 Timothy 1:10. It appears nowhere else in the First Testament or in Greek writings of Paul's era. It seems that Paul created the word for his purposes in this text. *Arsenokoitai* is made up of two parts: *arsen* means "man"; *koitai* means "beds." The word in English Bibles is interpreted as referring to homosexuals. Regardless of Paul's intent, translators have postulated a number of different English words for *arsenokoitai*: The KJV and ASV again are together with "abusers of themselves with mankind/men"; the NIV chooses "homosexual offenders"; the RSV renders it "sexual perverts"; the NRSV and NJB uses "sodomites," a pejorative perspective gleaned from a bad interpretation of Genesis 19:4-5. The traditional interpretation is that the term *arsenokoites* refers to male anal sex.

The exegetical points are the following:

✓ Two Greek words, *malakos* and *arsenokoites*, have given translators and interpreters headaches for 2000 years. The meaning of *malakos* is polyvalent; it can be translated a number of ways. Literally it means "soft," but it has been given sexual connotations by many translations. *Arsenokoites* is a word that Paul coined; it appears nowhere else in scripture or in contemporary Greek writing. It appears to be a word composed of two different words that appear in the Greek translation of the Hebrew scriptures called the Septuagint. Those two words translated literally are "bed" and "man."

✓ It is very possible that the two words refer to the common pederast relationship in the Greek culture. The first term refers to the young boy who is the sex object of the older man. This is exploitive sex, which we hold to be immoral as well, heterosexual or homosexual.

✓   Another very possible translation of the two words is prostitution, which is immoral for several reasons.

✓   Even if the words refer to male same-sex eroticism, it is unclear which particular male-male sexual relationships Paul refers to. The 10 Commandments outlaw murder, but in which cases does this commandment apply? We allow for lethal force under some circumstances of self-defense and war. Some cases of opposite-sex intercourse are immoral (rape, adultery, out of marriage) and some cases are not immoral. Commitment within a marriage is not immoral and is a gift from God. That is true regardless of sexual orientation.

✓   What about the rest of the list of "wrongdoers"? We scapegoat the LGBT community and ignore those categories that we do not fully understand and/or need to discuss.

EXEGETICAL ANALYSIS

Gagnon, the anti-LGBT author who does the most complete and thorough job trying to prove that the Bible condemns same-sex eroticism, translates *malakoi* as "effeminate males who play the sexual role of females."[95] The literal meaning of the word is soft or effeminate and can refer to clothing, objects, etc. Since there is a broad meaning of the word in Greek literature, Gagnon posits that its meaning is somewhere between "only prostituting passive homosexuals" and "effeminate heterosexual and homosexual males."[96] Gagnon's case that *malakos* instead, refers to effeminate males (penetrated) having sex with penetrators is somewhat based on his interpretation of *arsenokoites*, which is questionable.

One of Gagnon's warrants for his translation/interpretation is based on Philo, a Jewish contemporary of Paul's, who used the word *malakoi* (softness or effeminacy) alongside *anandria* (unmanliness) to refer to the behavior of passive homosexual partners (*hoi pas-*

---

95   Gagnon, p. 306.
96   Gagnon, p. 308.

chontes) who cultivate feminine features. However, the paragraph in Philo's Special Laws 3.37-42, referenced by Gagnon, describes boys who have taken on traditional feminine dress, cosmetics, jewelry, perfumes, curled hair, and behavior. They lead festival parades, and in some cases castrate themselves. Their behavior is condemned because they give up their proper roles as men, and take on the inferior role of women. The penetrator is condemned for destroying a boy, who now becomes as a woman, and for wasting seed that could be used for procreation with a woman. What Philo describes is akin to pederasty combined with some type of cultic/cultural observances; it could be temple prostitution. He does not describe what we might understand as homoerotic relationship. While some same-sex partners may cultivate feminine characteristics, some heterosexuals do as well. Why didn't Paul use *hoi paschontes* if he wanted to refer to passive partners in male-male eroticism? Gagnon's argument is also based on his belief that Paul in 1 Corinthians is referring to the admonitions in Leviticus. However, we do not know what, if anything, Paul is referring to in this text.

Gagnon translates *arsenokoitai* as "males who take other males to bed." He argues that *arsenokoites* was probably coined from two words that appear in the Septuagint translations of Leviticus 18:22 and 20:13 that condemn lying "with a male as with a woman." The two words are *arsenos* (for male) and a form of *koiten* (for bed or to lie). Hence, the compound word could mean "to lie with a male." Of course, this leaves out the term from Leviticus that has been wrongly translated as "as with a woman." Gagnon also recounts similar words used in the Hebrew by rabbis. However, rabbinical Judaism postdates Paul.

Gagnon quotes a number of non-canonical sources that use the word *arsenokoites* or a different form of the root word. Gagnon notes that there are lists of vices containing the word *arsenokoites*, similar to Paul's lists in his letters, in the Sibylline Oracles. However, the Sibylline Oracles are a chaotic mix of verses of unknown origins that were reworked over the centuries with the last redaction occurring about the 6th century CE. In none of these is the word actually defined. Since it appears with lists of vices of economic exploitation, it probably refers to prostitution. Similarly Gagnon sources the appearance of *arsenokoites* in a list of vices appearing in the *Acts of John* (2nd century CE). The word is not defined and the remainder of the list contains economic sins, not sexual sins. An early Christian writer, Theophilus of Antioch, uses the word in two different lists of vices that Gagnon quotes, but neither time is the word defined. One list contains economic issues, and in the second it appears between sexual and economic vices. It could refer to sexual exploitation. Several very significant patristic Christian writers such as Origen, Theodoret of Cyrrhus (450 CE), Cyril of Alexandria, and Nilus of Ancyra (ca. 410 CE) use *arsenokoites* in lists with *porneia* (sexual immorality) and *moicheia* (adultery), but *arsenokoitai* is still not explicated. Besides, these writers all lived a number of years after 1 Corinthians was written by Paul. We still do not know what Paul meant.

Gagnon refers to the 4th century Christian writer Eusebius in his *Preparation for the Gospel*, where the 2nd-3rd century Bardesanes is quoted using the word *arsenokoites* with a parenthetical definition: "wise men who have male lovers." However, it is not clear from the Greek text that the parenthetical expression refers to *arsenokoites*. Gagnon also points to Eusebius in his *Demonstration of the Gospel*, where he uses *arsenokoites* in a list of commands (presumably from Moses) where it occurs right after adultery. Elsewhere in the same work, "Moses" condemns by the following phrase: "males not be mad for males." However, even though Eusebius could be condemning male-male sex, there is no linkage to the word *arsenokoites*. Hence, these are the opinions of a 4th-century writer, not the Bible.

Gagnon also quotes John of Damascus, one the Doctors of the Church and recognized as one of the greatest theologians of all time. In John's work entitled *Sacra Parallela*, he links *arsenokoites* to the Leviticus 20:13, which is evidence that he believes the word refers to male-male sex. However, John died in 749 CE, so his opinion of what Paul meant by a word that Paul invented is moot.

The change in the Greek language alone is significant over a 700 year period.

Gagnon does relate to earlier sources such as the apostolic fathers. In lists from Barnabas 19:4, The *Didache 2:2*, Clement of Alexandria, Origen, and *The Apostolic Constitution* appear the Greek words *porneia* (fornication), *moicheia* (adultery), and *paidophthoria* (corruption of boys) parallel to lists of *porneia*, *moicheia*, and *arsenokoites*. Actually, this disclosure argues against Gagnon because one could assume that *arsenokoites* meant pederasty (*paidophthoria*). I looked up *Didache 2:2*, and the only comparable English word was pederasty.

The translation of *arsenokoites* has been difficult for hundreds of years. More recent translations are influenced by significant presuppositions that scapegoat and oppress the LGBT community.

Although Richard B. Hays is against LGBT inclusion and believes that *arsenokoitai* refers to generic male-male eroticism, he interprets *malakoi* narrowly as the boy who is engaged in a pederast association with an older man, based on Greek cultural usage of the word.[97] This is an interesting contradiction. Those who translate the first term of the pair (*malakos*) as the passive partner (victim?) in a pederast relationship generally would interpret the second term (*arsenokoitai*) as the active person in the pederast relationship. One follows the other. Yet, Hays translates *arsenokoitai* as encompassing all of male-male eroticism and *malakoi* as narrowly referring only to pederast relationships.

Gordon Fee, who has written a magnificent commentary on 1 Corinthians, has a more evangelical approach to the letter. His commentary addresses the ambiguities of the text and some of the history of its exegesis. He concludes the following:

> The next two words, however, translated "male prostitutes" and "homosexual offenders" in the NIV, require considerable comment. The first word, *malakoi*, has the basic meaning of "soft"; but it also became a pejorative epithet for men who were "soft" or "effeminate," most likely referring to the young-

---

97   Hays, p. 97.

er, "passive" partner in a pederastic relationship—the most common form of homosexuality in the Greco-Roman world.[98]

Fee notes that the word *arsenokoitai* is more difficult because it is unique. It is a compound word composed of "male" and crude slang for sexual intercourse. Hence, it could refer to males who have intercourse (male prostitutes of all kinds) or those who have intercourse with males (homosexuals).[99] The meaning is ambiguous, but Fee thinks that the NIV version is close to correct, so that *malakoi* refers to male prostitutes (specifically a consenting homosexual youth) and *arsenokoitai* refers more broadly to homosexual offenders. However, I note the term "consenting homosexual youth" is anachronistic. Paul's culture had no understanding of homosexuality as an orientation. On the other hand, if *malakoi* refers to male prostitution, we would agree that all prostitution is immoral.

Fee is not very clear on *arsenokoitai*. What is a "homosexual offender"? The term implies orientation, which was unknown by Paul. Does Fee mean the penetrator in homoeroticism? Or does he mean the person who has sex with the young homosexual prostitute? If so, we would agree that prostitution is immoral. In any case Fee is not really very clear on his exegesis at this point.

Craig Keener is convinced that *arsenokoites* refers to generic homosexual activity because the two root words that make it up appear in the Septuagint in Leviticus 20:13, and they refer to males lying with males.[100] Keener agrees with the others that *malakos* refers to the younger man in the pederastic relationship. Keener's exegesis of the list ignores the order in which the two Greek words appear.

In his commentary on 1 Corinthians from the *New Interpreters Bible* (NIB), Sampley very briefly points out the difficulties with translation of the two Greek words. He is not completely conclusive, but he does seem to favor the pederasty interpretation: "Obviously, it [*malaokos*] would have been applied to the young

---

98   Fee, p. 243.
99   Fee, p. 244.
100   Keener, p. 54.

boy involved with an older man. The second term was applied to men who engaged in pederasty or were sodomite; accordingly, the term was used to describe the more active male."[101] Sampley describes the culture that supported pederasty as very exploitative, although there were instances where it was the *malakoi* who solicited sex with older men. Paul's complete list of vices is "part of his general critique of the way non-believers behave."[102] Interestingly, the NIB commentary is presumably neutral in its interpretation, yet Sampley seems to clearly prefer the inclusive opinion that Paul is not talking about all homoeroticism. Perhaps it is his own understanding of the context of Paul's letter; after all, Paul is writing to the mostly Greek Corinthian church that was having some sexual morality issues. Pederasty was a part of that culture and it belongs in Paul's list of sins.

Furnish, a leading expert on Pauline literature, takes a very different tack from others in his interpretation of *malakoi* and *arsenokoitai*. He establishes the difficulty of determining what Paul meant by the two words and summarizes the possible interpretations. However, he ends up translating them broadly as homoerotic behavior, with a caveat at the end.

> It is possible, then, to take *malakoi* as a reference to "male prostitutes" (e.g., NRSV) and *arsenokoitai* as a reference to males who pay to have sex with them. But it is equally possible, and probably better, to take the words as referring, respectively, to the "receptive" and "aggressive" males in any homoerotic encounter. We may therefore translate the first term as "effeminate males," and the second as "males who have sex with males." Our next task is to consider the context in which these references occur.[103]

Within the greater context of Paul's theology and Christology, both this text and the Roman's text discussed earlier serve the same purpose. According to Furnish, this list and other lists in the

101 Sampley, p. 859.
102 Sampley, p. 859.
103 Furnish, p. 80.

Pauline letters are vices and not sins, per se. Paul understands "sin" as singular, not the plural "sins." Sin is the power that separates humankind from God, and the Christ event is what overcomes the power of sin. These vices are symptomatic of sin, and these symptoms are evidence of sin within and controlling all people. Paul's overarching theme is that the Corinthians used to be enslaved by sin and exhibited various vices, and now they were different because of Christ. Paul is making no moral case against homoerotic behavior.

John Boswell, on the other hand, holds that there is no connection between the two words. I think he has a point because the second text from 1 Timothy has *arsenokoitai* in its list without the word *malakos*. Whoever wrote 1 Timothy in Paul's name did not perceive the two words as linked. Boswell does not spend much time on these two words, simply because no one really knows for sure what Paul meant. We may wish that he had been clearer, but we only have what he wrote, not what we would have him write. Boswell points out the plethora of possible translations of *malakos*, a very common word in the Greek Scriptures (NT) and the patristic writings. It translated as sick, liquid, cowardly, refined, weak-willed, delicate, gentle, and debauched. In a moral context it frequently means licentious or wanting in self-control. It is not paired in any way with homoerotic sex anywhere in the Greek world. *Arsenokoites*, as Boswell notes, is very rare, and its application to homosexuality is more understandable. However, Boswell notes that it did not mean homosexuality, that to Paul's contemporaries it "meant 'male prostitute' until well into the fourth century, after which it became confused with a variety of words for disapproved sexual activity and was often equated with homosexuality."[104] Taken in the context of 1 Corinthians, Boswell suggests that it could mean loose, wanton, unrestrained, or undisciplined. Hence, it does not necessarily have any relation to sex acts of any type. Boswell suggests that *arsenokoitai* refers to male prostitutes who were available to men or women.

---

104 Boswell, p. 107.

Jack Rogers takes the high road regarding these two words. He describes the work of Dale Martin on the word *arsenokoites* that indicates some kind of economic exploitation related to sex, such as rape, prostitution, pimping, or the like. There is no clear evidence that it refers to male-male eroticism. *Malakos* means soft and probably refers to effeminacy, which was a moral category in Paul's day but not today.

Helminiak reviews the literal meaning of *malakos* plus the interpretation put on it by various Bible translations and scholars and then summarizes his own position as follows: *Malakos* could be translated as "effeminate" but there is no real reason (other than bias) to link it with homosexuality; it could also describe men who primped themselves to attract women or men who were lazy or loose as a contrast to virile or manly.[105] The word "wimp" occurs to me. Being a wimp is not a moral sin, but it sure is shameful to some in our culture; or maybe it is a sin if the "wimp" does not provide for his family because he is lazy.

Helminiak notes that the two root words for *arseno-* and *koitai* appear in the Septuagint in Leviticus 18:22 and 20:13 in the phrase "the man who lies with a male the lyings of a woman." Therefore, it is possible that *arsenokoitai* refers back to those texts and means the active participant in male-male eroticism. However, Helminiak interprets Paul's list as one that addresses issues that existed in the Roman culture of the first century (Corinth was a Roman town). It was a decadent society filled with moral decadence: for example, pederasty, prostitution, kidnapping of girls and boys and selling them into sexual slavery, sexual lust, and sexual exploitation in general. I understand Helminiak to mean that Paul was addressing a laundry list of vices that were present in Corinth, including exploitative male-male homoeroticism.

Helminiak notes that an earlier work by Robin Scroggs[106] proposed that the two words function together as the penetrated and the penetrator in anal sex act. Scroggs understands the word *mala-*

---

105   Helminiak, pp. 108-109.
106   Robin Scroggs, *The New Testament and Homosexuality* (1983).

kos to mean "effeminate call boy," a young person selling his body to another male, or an active participant in pederasty. Therefore, the active man, the *arsenokoitai*, and the passive, or *malakos*, boy are both condemned by Paul. In summary, we do not know what point Paul was trying to make in his list with these two words.

Many traditionalists translate *arsenokoitai* as something like "a man who has intercourse with another man." This translation is based on the etymology of the word that is a compound made up of *arseno-* or man and koitai, crude slang for sex. Countryman points out the danger of translating New Testament Greek based only on etymology instead of usage. He provides an interesting example in the English language: "outbuilding" and "outhouse" have similar etymology and should mean the same thing, but their conventional usage says something very different. An outbuilding is barn, shed, garage, shop, and the like some distance from the main house. An outhouse is a latrine. Dale Martin has proposed some similar linguistics regarding compound words. Take two words like "under" and "stand," which we "understand" as something very different when put together.

Countryman believes the two words are jointly related to sex and money since the word immediately before these two is adultery and the word after is about stealing; so they bridge the meaning between sex and money. Countryman suggests that *arsenokoitai* means a male prostitute who cultivates the elderly in order to inherit their estates.

In the section on "property," instead of "purity" (these two themes describe Countryman's typology for understanding sexual ethics in the Bible), Paul places these two words, and other sexual mores, into the property ethic. Countryman thinks that Paul's reasoning behind sexual mores in the Corinthian letter is related to property rather than purity. The entire Chapter 5 is devoted to the narrative and condemnation of the man living with his "mother," which is a violation of property rights vis-à-vis the incest rules in the Leviticus. 1 Corinthians 7:15 sort of fits this typology since Paul condemns prostitution because Christians belong to Christ, and messing with prostitutes is infringing on Christ's property rights.

> *15 Do you not know that your bodies are members of Christ? Should I therefore take the members of Christ and make them members of a prostitute? Never! 16 Do you not know that whoever is united to a prostitute becomes one body with her? For it is said, "The two shall be one flesh." 17 But anyone united to the Lord becomes one spirit with him.*

Similarly, Paul recognizes that both men and women are capable of committing adultery because the two "own" each other, and violating the covenant is an infringement on property rights.

Powell basically concurs with the traditionalist interpretation of the two words. He acknowledges the ambiguities of *arsenokoitai* and its alleged pairing with *malakos*, but agrees that they could refer to the effeminate male who allows himself to be penetrated by another male. However, his spin is that we are unsure of what male-male sex is being referred to: "In short, the condemnations of *arsenokoitai* and *malakoi* in these texts may imply that generally speaking, men who have sex with other men are acting in a way that is not pleasing to God, but such condemnations do not disallow instances in which men who have sex with each other are not behaving as *arsenokoitai* and or *malakoi*."[107] I think what Powell is saying is that there are contextual circumstances for every act. The Ten Commandments condemn murder, but an ordered society recognizes the necessity of self-defense with lethal force under some extenuating circumstances. Legally and morally, killing someone is not always murder. Although Paul is condemning *arsenokoitai* and *malakos*, both of which could refer to male-male eroticism, not all male-male eroticism involves *arsenokoitai* and *malakos*. We just don't know what Paul means by the two words. He could be referring to pederasty, prostitution, exploitive sex, etc. It is certain that he did not have the knowledge of homosexual orientation.

---

107 Powell, p. 26.

Alexander's take on *arsenokoitai* and *malakos* is somewhat similar to Powell's, in which *malakos* simply means "soft," but since *malakos* are not going to enter the kingdom of heaven, it must mean someone who is "bad." Within the context of the Greco-Roman culture that Paul is addressing, pederasty was quite prevalent. *Malakoi* could be referring to "catamites" or boys kept by older men for unnatural purposes. Alexander notes the difficulty of interpreting *arsenokoitai* that every other scholar has had, but he does think it has to do with male same-sex eroticism. Like Powell, he does not think it is possible to know what specific sex act Paul had in mind with this word, whether pederasty or other acts. He offers his own interpretation that *arsenokoitai* is best translated into English as "sexual perverts."

So what conclusions can we draw from Paul's writings in 1 Corinthians, specifically the list with the two words *arsenokoitai* and *malakos*?

✓ *Malakos* is a common word in the Greek world of Paul's era. It literally means "soft" and can and has been translated a number of ways. It could refer to some effeminate behavior such as the passive young partner in a pederast relationship. Such a relationship would be considered morally wrong today.

✓ *Arsenokoitai* could possibly refer to male-male sex acts, or not. If it does, it is not at all clear which sex acts could or not could not be involved. Paul could be referring to all male-male sex acts, but more likely specific ones that were affecting the Corinthian church. Those acts could have included pederasty, prostitution, orgy sex events of all kinds, exploitative sex involving money, abuse, or slavery, and the like.

✓ What is really fascinating about the utilization of this particular text is how the rest of the list of "wrongdoers" is completely and totally ignored. Society, some churches, and some governments have denied and still deny rights and grace to committed homosexuals, but adultery has been given celebrity status in our media. If the church were to exclude all of those in Paul's list as it has excluded gays (the exclusion is not universal of all churches or of all of society and government) then there would be no church. It is beyond the scope of this paper to address the prevalence of adultery and fornication, but my perception is that it is widespread and accepted by the church in general.

THE APOSTLE PAUL ON HOMOSEXUALITY: TIMOTHY

9) 1 Timothy 1:8 *Now we know that the law is good, if one uses it legitimately.* *⁹ This means understanding that the law is laid down not for the innocent but for the lawless and disobedient, for the godless and sinful, for the unholy and profane, for those who kill their father or mother, for murderers, ¹⁰ fornicators, sodomites, slave traders, liars, perjurers, and whatever else is contrary to the sound teaching ¹¹ that conforms to the glorious gospel of the blessed God, which he entrusted to me.*

Written at a later date than 1 Corinthians, by a person using Paul's name, 1 Timothy also contains the Paulism *arsenokoites* in a list of items that describe those who are lawless, disobedient, godless, sinful, unholy, and profane. It presents the same translation problems here that it does in 1 Corinthians. Again the NRSV translates it as sodomites, a pejorative translation. The use by this author destroys the interpreters of 1 Corinthians 6:9 who translate the paired words *malakos* and *arsenokoitai* as the penetrated and penetrator in male-male anal sex. At least by the time of epistle of 1 Timothy, *arsenokoitai* stood alone in its meaning. If the order of the list was thought out by the writer, it is interesting to note that it appears between *porneia* (fornicators) and slave traders. It could refer to some kind of exploitative sex.

WHAT WOULD JESUS SAY IF HE WERE ASKED?

The entire argument over homoeroticism focuses on scriptures that are *not* in the gospels of Matthew, Mark, Luke, or John. Jesus is not quoted as saying anything about homoeroticism. Some have tried to extrapolate what he thought of the subject based on his general teachings. Gagnon has a short chapter entitled *The Witness of Jesus*,[108] where he states that Jesus was against same-sex intercourse for several reasons: 1) Jesus' general approach to the Mosaic Law; 2) His discourse on divorce and adultery; 3) His rigorous approach to sexual ethics; and 4) Jesus did not ever overturn any specific prohibition of the law.

Jack Rogers puts a completely different spin on the personhood of Jesus. While Jesus says nothing about the acceptance of gays into full covenant with him, his teachings and actions indicate that he would accept them: The parable of the Good Samaritan (Luke 10:25-37), the acceptance of sexual minorities such as the eunuchs (Mathew 19:10-12), and he also counseled mutuality in marriage that was decidedly patriarchic in his day (Matthew 19:3-9). Jesus consistently subverted the patriarchal religious and social hierarchy and extended egalitarian welcome to everyone, not just the privileged few at the top of the social order.

I perceive that it is difficult to know why Jesus did not say anything about homoeroticism. There is a plethora of possible explanations:

1. Some things that Jesus commented on were in response to questions. The parable of the Good Samaritan was answering the question "Who is my neighbor"? The discourse on divorce and adultery was preceded by a question regarding the lawfulness of divorce. The question regarding the paying of taxes to an occupying force (the Romans) was answered by "Give therefore to the emperor the things that are the emperor's, and to God the things that are God's" (Matthew 22:21). In each of these question and answer sections, Jesus

---

108 Gagnon, pp. 185-210.

extended the thinking of the people who asked by answering more deeply than the question itself. In the Gospel stories, no one ever asked Jesus about homoeroticism, so he never taught on the subject. This explanation is not that good because Jesus also taught many things that he was not asked about. The Sermon on the Mount is a good example (Matthew 4:25-7:29).

2.   Perhaps Jesus did say something about homoeroticism, but it did not make it into the written accounts. This explanation is a moot point. We only have what we have, and anything else is conjecture.

3.   Gagnon's explanation is that Jesus agreed with Mosaic Law; so whatever was Jewish Law was still valid. Indeed, Jesus was a Jewish man who followed Jewish Law ... sort of. However, he broke the traditional Sabbath Law that was based on one of the Ten Commandments and the Genesis account of creation when God rested on the 7th day. In the Sermon on the Mount, he replaced the law from Exodus (Exodus 21:24 a-b) that reads "eye for eye, tooth for tooth" with "Do not resist an evildoer. But if anyone strikes you on the right cheek, turn the other also" (Matthew 5:39b). So this explanation is not valid; Jesus abrogated or changed some laws and repeated other laws. Besides if Jesus came only to reinforce Jewish Law, then what does it mean to be a Christian? While we honor our Abrahamic heritage, we do not practice Judaism.

4.   Jesus would not have found it necessary to repeat what everyone else (he preached and taught Jews not Gentiles) already believed. However, Jesus found it necessary to repeat laws "that everyone already believed." For example, from Matthew 15 we have the following list: "For out of the heart come evil intentions, murder, adultery, fornication, theft, false witness, slander. These are what defile a person, but to eat with unwashed hands does not defile." Murder, adultery, and theft are all in the Ten Commandments, which Jesus repeats even though everyone agreed. When the so-called rich,

young ruler asked Jesus what he must do to inherit eternal life, part of Jesus' reply from Luke 20:19-20 is "You know the commandments: 'You shall not commit adultery; You shall not murder; You shall not steal; You shall not bear false witness; Honor your father and mother.'"[109] So if everybody believed homoeroticism was sinful, why didn't he repeat it?

5.　Perhaps Jesus did not know that homoeroticism existed, but this scenario is difficult to believe. Jesus lived a short distance from Sepphoris, a large Greek city, so even if the little town of Nazareth was unaware of the real world, Sepphoris would have exposed him to male-male intercourse,

6.　Jesus either did not think it was wrong or thought it not important enough to mention. Either explanation is basically the same thing. Jesus had about three years to get across crucial information through the spoken word, by actions such has feeding the 5000, and in metaphoric events such as walking on water or exorcising demons. Homoeroticism was not an important issue to Jesus... not important enough to mention.

The interesting thing is that Jesus did not explicitly mention a lot of things that are issues in our society; abortion, euthanasia, capital punishment, global warming, education, the environment, gun control, or health care. Many of these items were not part of his culture, and others he did not directly mention. Actually, he did not give a lot of rules and laws even when asked. When asked something, he often told a story (parable) or gave a much deeper response as noted in the gospel of John. I suggest that he did this on purpose to make us think and discern. This thinking is one part of the Wesley quadrilateral known as "reason." So how do we reason with what we have in the gospels?

To try to ascertain what Jesus said or would have said is almost as fruitless as another quest for the historical Jesus. Rather, it would seem to more useful to search the scriptures and search our own hearts through the lens of Jesus' life, death, and resurrection.

109　Similar story and list are given in Matthew 19:16-19 and Mark 10:18-19.

Jesus was a radical Jew because he was totally inclusive in his life. Although his famous head-butting with the Pharisees and other people of authority was due to his very radical teaching, it was also due to his constant schmoozing with the "wrong" people. He hung out with tax collectors, Samaritans, lepers, children, strange women off of the street, Roman soldiers, Gentiles (Syro-Phoenician woman), and his disciples were not men of religious distinction. Jesus welcomed everyone. The parable of the Good Samaritan is especially radical in its inclusiveness. The woman accused of adultery was let off of stoning by the crowd (What happened to the man involved with adultery?), a punishment reminiscent of Sharia Law today. On the other hand, she was told to "go and sin no more." Jesus definitely had a special place in his heart for the marginalized from and by society. The parable of "the least of these" (Matthew 25:31-46) should lead us to caution in excluding anyone from the Kingdom. Those who do not extend full privileges to the LGBT community would say that they are welcome, but if they are excluded from the same covenant benefits that heterosexuals enjoy, are they really welcome? If God created us for his love and companion love, demanding denial of that love (celibacy) from the LGBT community is inconsistent.

The majority of scholars who deny companionship rights to the LGBT community concede that LGBT orientation is a discovery, not a choice. Led by scholars such as Gagnon, they say that their orientation is a discovery, but they must remain celibate. They might add that "sin is sin." Jesus accepts all into the Kingdom, but there are certain requirements. Bank robbers are welcome, but they have to repent and quit robbing banks. Here's the rub. Bank robbers choose to rob banks; being gay is not a choice. There is a choice of sorts in acting upon the sexual urges most of us have. However, to deny physical, spiritual, psychological, and emotional covenantal support to a group created in the image of God is oppression.

PART 2: THE POSSIBILITY OF SCRIPTURAL
UNITY WITHIN THE
UNITED METHODIST CHURCH

MOVING FORWARD

Subsequent to writing most of the book I joined an organization entitled: *Breaking the Silence*,[110] a Texas Annual Conference United Methodist Church organization that advocates for the full inclusion the LGBT community within the United Methodist Church. This organization relates to the national organization called Reconciling Ministries Network that has the following mission: "Reconciling Ministries Network mobilizes United Methodists of all sexual orientations and gender identities to transform our Church and world into the full expression of Christ's inclusive love."[111] I mention these organizations because I have had the opportunity to fellowship with committed Christians who happen to be gay. While I had already come to the bible based conclusions that homoeroticism is not necessarily a sin, and gay marriage should be supported by the church, fellowshipping, dialoguing, and friending the total Christian community would be very beneficial for bishops, clergy, and members of the United Methodist Church; or any church for that matter.

Any forward program for the denomination should include the voice and participation of the LGBT community and intensive bible study. My exegesis and the exegesis of others certainly illustrate the varying conclusions reached. The question is not biblical authority. The question is biblical interpretation, and regardless of the interpretation the homoerotic issue is one of the very minority issues in the bible and Christianity.

I am old enough to remember the very early days of television. I never gave much thought to the fact that all or most of the people on Howdy Doody, Captain Kangaroo, The Mickey

---

110 http://www.btsumc.org/
111 http://www.rmnetwork.org/newrmn/

Mouse Club, The Sid Caesar Show, Ed Sullivan, Jackie Gleason, and many other shows were all white with rare exceptions! (where were the African-American mouseketeers?) Movies like *Gone with the Wind* or *The Little Rascals* typically displayed African-Americans in a negative light. When African-American actors first began to appear in shows and commercials it was very obvious. It was also disconcerting to a number of people who considered themselves non-racist. The sight of a black man kissing or hugging a white woman troubled a lot of people. (of course, in the days of Jim Crow a black man could be lynched for looking at a white woman). The days of racism are not over. Black Lives (really do) Matter, but many people have not caught on. After the dreadful shooting of nine African-Americans in a bible study in Charlestown, South Carolina, a person one block from my house hung up a rebel flag from his porch. However, many of us white people have moved on past Jim Crow attitudes, and seeing black actors or mixed couples in public or the media is no longer disturbing. We are making progress, but there is still much that needs to be accomplished before Martin Luther King's dream will come true.

I bring all of this up because I believe that many people have similar problems with the LGBT community that was (and is) prevalent in the Jim Crow era. For so long homosexuals had to remain in the closet or face extreme discrimination and abuse, so straights that experience out-of-the closet homosexuals expressing any display of affection react negatively. Along with recovering the meaning of scripture, there is a necessity of fellowshipping with the LGBT community. I think we straights have developed an prejudicial, internal "yuck" factor directed towards all LGBT people. Even some of us who say we are inclusive and welcoming to the LGBT community are unable to accord them sexual satisfaction and love that God has provided us all. The "love the sin and hate the sinner" aphorism is a tragic misunderstanding of what sin is when it is applied to those in the LGBT community who are in committed relationships.

Some UMC congregations could have difficulty accepting a gay or lesbian pastor. Of course, some still have difficulty accepting a woman pastor or supporting a multiethnic initiative. Yet, it seems that once a congregation becomes used to a gay pastor, the fact that he or she is homosexual does not seem to matter to the congregation. The recent case of the AME pastor Benjamin Hutchinson who was fired from a UMC church by the district leaders of Cassiopolis, Michigan, appears to have upset the congregation that he served. They were suspicious when he came three years ago, but they have learned to appreciate his ministry.[112] It is relatively easy to hold negative opinions of a class of people and more difficult when you actually know them.

Regardless of proving the case in scripture, the United Methodist Church and other denominations are confused and foundering over the issue of homosexuality. We are all struggling at the administrative, judicatory, and local church levels. A short book edited by the late Bishop Rueben P. Job and publisher Neil M. Alexander has tried to point the way forward for the United Methodist Church by enlisting seven other UMC bishops to write essays from various perspectives on the LGBT crisis in the UMC. The title of the book is *Finding Our Way: Love and Law in the United Methodist Church*, and the various essays/chapters are entitled "Enforce" by Gregory V. Palmer, "Emend" by Hope Morgan Ward, "Disobey" by Melvin G. Talbert, "Disarm" by Kenneth H. Carter, "Order" by J. Michael Lowry, "Unity" by John K. Yambasu, "Diversity" by Rosemarie Wenner, and "Trust God" by Rueben P. Job. While each of these essays was written for the benefit of the UMC, they could easily have applicability to a broader audience. This same group is engaged in panel discussions that are available online. If there is a shortcoming in this series of essays, it is the missing voices from the LGBT community. However, it is a welcome attempt to keep the denomination unified, which is getting more and more difficult.

---

112   http://www.wsbt.com/news/local/i-wont-hide-from-it-gay-pastor-al-legedly-forced-to-resign-from-local-church/34166340

A very interesting story about the North Carolina Conference of the UMC is told by Bishop Ward.[113] The North Carolina Conference established a Unity Dialogue of 25 members that began meeting in August of 1998 to wrestle with the LGBT "issue." The process is described in some detail and included witnesses, panel discussions, break-out groups, holy communion, and preaching. They earnestly studied the so-called clobber verses discussed in this book. She describes a long, arduous process that was initiated and led by then Bishop Marion Edwards. The meetings included a diverse group of witnesses from the LGBT community; LGBT people and family members of LGBT people. The process included intense Bible study and listening to the voices of the LGBT community to understand their Christian commitments and prejudices directed at them.

In 2013 the North Carolina Conference approved a resolution calling on the General Conference to change the language in the Social Principles of the United Methodist Discipline to affirm the place of LGBT persons. It obviously took many years for that particular conference to get through the issue to a scripturally based endpoint, and I think the scriptural study is a key part of their discernment. For anyone or any group that is grappling with similar discernment, witnesses from the LGBT community and their relatives are crucial in putting human faces on this issue, but Bible study is also essential. No matter how much love exists towards the LGBT community, poorly interpreted scripture can still scapegoat them. Perhaps this book should have been named *Love versus Law* instead of *Love and Law*. What exists in the UMC is language put in the "law" (UMC Discipline) in 1972 that is being held up against scripture.

Bishop Melvin Talbert has been instrumental in pushing the discernment process by an act of Discipline disobedience in performing a gay wedding. He has received a lot of abuse and some affirmation for his actions. His essay is worth reading to see how he came to believe, to speak out, and to officiate at a gay wedding.

---

113 Job, pp. 20-23.

He does not address the so-called clobber verses but takes a stand on scripture versus the Discipline:

> To be clear, the language regarding marriage (paragraph 161B) and regarding homosexuality (paragraph 161F) is not found in scripture and does not account for the contemporary understanding of who LGBT people understand themselves to be. And the discriminatory laws prohibiting clergy and congregations from being in full and inclusive ministry to and with LGBT people (paragraph 3441.6) are oppressive and conflict with other sections of the Book of Discipline, which urge congregations to be in full ministry to all persons and urge parents not to condemn or abandon their children who are gay and lesbian.[114]

Although the writers make some attempts to present the particular subject that they have been given in a neutral way, that proves to be very difficult. Also, the bishops are charged with keeping the church together even if that comes at the cost of oppressing a minority LGBT community. That does not mean that they willfully oppress anyone, but it is a fine line to walk, trying to keep everyone engaged with differing viewpoints. And viewpoints, even including the role of scripture, are decidedly different among the bishops themselves. Bishop Yambasu has an unusual position: "I believe that the Bible is the infallible word of God. The Bible provides direction for all those who proclaim Christ as their Lord and Savior. I believe, therefore, that sexual promiscuity, homosexuality, and adultery are inconsistent with the teachings of scripture."[115] The United Methodist Church does not teach that the Bible is the infallible word of God.

Bishop Carter does not recommend schism within the UMC but touches on the eventual possibility of a schism between three groups: progressive (Reconciling; The Methodist Federation for Social Action; Breaking the Silence), evangelical (no denominational label; Willow Creek Association; larger churches; Confessing;

---

114 Job, p. 45.
115 Job, p. 87.

Good News), and mainstream (most connectional and aligned with our present structure).[116] This is all hypothetical but makes some sense if the LGBT issue continues to cripple our ability to do mission for the least of these in the name of the Lord. Perhaps, these three groups could still be serviced by a central group containing some of the current organizations such as Cokesbury and Abingdon. We could share facilities and preachers across loosely defined boundaries. There is a good article at www.UMC.org that discusses the pros and cons of an amicable separation and some of the advocates from both sides.[117]

The major difficulty in bringing together disparate groups and individuals within the UMC is biblical understanding or lack thereof. I am in agreement with Adam Hamilton, one of the great preachers and teachers of our generation. He has written many books containing first-class scholarship in an easy-to-read format for laity and clergy. Several of these books broach divisive issues within the church, including homosexuality. A recent book, *Making Sense of the Bible*, contains Chapter 29 on homosexuality. At the end of the chapter, Hamilton states that "Ultimately the key to finding our way forward on this issue will come from our ability to articulate a clear view of scripture that recognizes both its divine inspiration and its humanity."[118] This would be good book to bring to a Bible-based dialogue that would cover a number of different issues within the church: science versus religion, theodicy, Christology, feminism, homosexuality, and many other topics. The concept of the book is to teach Christians how to get as much out of the Bible as possible. I heartily recommend this book by Hamilton for study groups throughout the United Methodist Church. I just used it in a study group at a sister United Methodist nearby, and it generated some interesting discussion. Hopefully, it generated a motivation to more and careful reading of scripture, which is Adam Hamilton's goal in writing the book. People think they know what the bible

116   Job, p. 68.
117   http://www.umc.org/news-and-media/amicable-breakup-of-umc-needed-pastor-group-says
118   Hamilton, *Making Sense*, p. 279.

says, but many do not. They also read it through presupposition lens that lead to bad exegesis. That does not mean that we all have to interpret something the same way, but it would lead to fruitful discussions rather than harsh attacks.

A study of this book could lead into an ongoing discernment modeled after the North Carolina Conference. That does not mean that all Conferences would come to the same conclusions, but that churches and individuals within each conference would learn where they stand and where other churches and individuals stand. It might even help us to understand each other's viewpoints. If such a discernment methodology does not result in unity, it would provide the boundaries for considering an amicable division. Contingent casualties would occur within local churches that are somewhat unexposed to the current argument. One of the difficulties in deciding the facilitation and/or teaching is the mechanism for putting the groups together and deciding on leadership. Also, clergy who have been educated at the very same seminary and in the same class of instruction have drawn completely different conclusion from the same scripture. No one is challenging the authority of scripture, but we interpret it differently.

I once had a very wise, albeit young, professor of Old Testament at Perkins School of Theology, Dr. Roy Heller. I can quote him verbatim: "The only thing you cannot learn is what you already know." He noted that when people met him in places such as on an airplane, they always want to ask him some question about the creation narratives in Genesis. His answer is always, "I don't know; let's take a look." The gist of this bit of wisdom is that people think that they know scripture, but they really do not. I think people form presuppositions about scripture based on casual biblical readings, something they remember from Sunday school years earlier, or verbiage from others such as "Homosexuality is an abomination, it says so in the Bible." So, scripture study is the key.

Unfortunately, the bishops on the Council of Bishops of the United Methodist Church disagree on the whether to accept gay marriages and/or unions. They are struggling among themselves with the "issue" that presents as several difficult conundrums:

- ✓ Our culture has oppressed the LGBT community for many years, but society's perception is changing faster than the United Methodist Church.

- ✓ Prior to the changing mores in society that were oppressing the LGBT community, it was convenient for pastors to speak with great authority against the minority. Thundering against a minority is a way of avoiding uncomfortable sermons for the majority. Simply ignore or play down the necessity of serving the common good of all people by beating on those without a voice.

- ✓ Lay people are caught in a vice of paradigms created by repeated but wrong social norms and repeated but wrong doctrine derived from non-contextual exegesis.

- ✓ The bishops themselves have differences of opinion regarding scriptural interpretation. Bishop Yambasu believes that scripture is the infallible word of God, which is decidedly biblical teaching at odds with the Methodist Discipline. They can hardly lead the church when they cannot agree among themselves.

- ✓ The overarching mission of the Council of Bishops is to preserve United Methodist Church unity. At all costs they must preserve unity. If they support one side or the other, they could have a schism on their hands, which they would regard as a total failure of their mission.

- ✓ On the other hand, the bishops need to do something. Some regard this issue as comparable to the argument and schism over slavery. Are we heading toward schism?

- ✓ The church and culture did suffer during the Jim Crow years, the civil rights era, desegregation, white supremacy, and the KKK era. We still do deal with more insidious racism. Yet, in spite of all this historic and present head-butting, we do survive and continue to move forward. So it is possible to avoid schism.

- ✓ Time. Some pastors have pushed the envelope by performing same-sex ceremonies. The bishops should have taken action long ago as did the North Carolina Conference. The bishops do not have the luxury of coming to an agreement among themselves before the church needs to come to a resolution.

- ✓ The compromise that has been suggested that allows both actions to exist side-by-side[119] will not work to maintain a single denomination. That is to say, some churches and pastors will allow gay marriages and/or unions and some will decide not to. Revs. Mike Slaughter and Adam Hamilton took a lot of heat for suggesting this compromise, which was intended to keep the UMC from splitting.

- ✓ Regardless of the action taken, there will be problems associated with the issue for many years. There are still churches reluctant to accept women pastors; there are few cross-ethnic appointments; there are some churches a long way from integration. These issues were settled long ago at General Conference, but they still exist in society and the church.

The real issue is biblical interpretation. How does one read and interpret the Bible? Just to say that we should follow what it says does not work. Salem, Massachusetts, did that and burned "witches" at the stake. Women who have followed Abraham's example of sacrificing a child have been tried as murderers. The Methodist Episcopal Church split at General Conference in 1844 over the issue of slavery, although both sides claimed scriptural warrants for

---

119 The Mike Slaughter/Adam Hamilton amendment, http://umcconnections.org/2012/05/03/hamiltonslaughter-substitution-related-to-ci-513/, that was presented to the General Conference in 2012 was basically a call to agree to disagree. It failed to pass. The complete document is at http://awayforward.net/.

their claims. Yet, with the current issue, both sides claim scriptural warrants.

I admire and appreciate the attempt by Revs. Slaughter and Hamilton to broach a compromise by allowing individual churches and/or conferences to decide for themselves what to believe and practice regarding homosexual marriage. However, there are two issues with this approach. Some think that it does not adhere to our episcopacy model and turns us into congregationalists. I seriously doubt that is the case because we have a lot of different beliefs and practices in local churches. We seemed to do okay before the non-inclusion clause was added in 1972. Was that clause written by the hand of God? Secondly, is it just to allow the noninclusion clause to exist? Is it just to allow discrimination to exist at all within the doctrine of the church? Would we allow the doctrine to discriminate against ethnic or racial groups or women? Would we allow various churches to discriminate against ethnic or racial groups or women? We might allow it because churches are made up of sinners, but we would not condone it by putting it in the doctrine. The noninclusion clause needs to come out of the Discipline. We have no similar clauses for divorcees, those having sex outside of marriage, slanderers, abortion, the wealthy, liars, etc.

What now? This book has been mostly about the biblical interpretation of the clobber verses. Within the laity and clergy of the church there are two myths that prevent getting to the Bible study. In fact, Bible study is step three. Steps one and two are the dispelling of two myths. Myth 1: Homosexuality is a lifestyle choice. This myth is still amazingly prevalent even today. The Phil Robertson statements presuppose that a heterosexual man, for some reason, has sex with a man rather than a woman. Myth 2: Homosexual people are promiscuous and in some sense very sick, demented, or abnormal. This belief (or beliefs) is based on ignorance of what homosexuality is. However, many of the caricatures of gay people running around in parades half naked with purple hair do not represent gay people any more than heterosexuals doing the same thing represent all straight people.

So a forward program must initially dispel nonbiblical myths as well as biblical myths of interpretation ... but how?

1) All of the elders of the church (including bishops; they are elders) will attend mandatory training within their respective conferences. They will listen to medical professionals explain to them what homosexuality is and everything that science knows about it.

2) At this same training, representatives from the LGBT community will tell their personal stories, including their faith journeys. The intent is not to raise sympathy but illustrate that LGBT people are just like straight people. These two steps are intended to eliminate presuppositions based on ignorance. The Church has to hear the voices of LGBT people; especially those living within committed, Christian relationships. It would be especially useful to hear from LGBT who are ordained clergy within the UMC or other denominations.

3) At this point of the training, each conference will have representatives from their closest UMC seminary to discuss the clobber verses and other biblical warrants regarding LGBT community relationship. This will require at least one First Testament scholar, one Pauline scholar, and a scholar with expertise on the gospels. These scholars must be from one of the 13 UMC seminaries. Seminary professors that I had at Perkins would be able to give a thoughtful, balanced report. These presentations should focus on biblical interpretation. Specific content would be up to the presenters. The intent is for clergy to understand what the Bible has to say (or not say) about homosexuality.

The three steps above involve a tremendous expenditure of connectional resources. Clergy will be upset about having to sit through these materials for a variety of reasons. Some will regard it as heretical, some as redundant to their knowledge, and some as not being helpful to their ministry. However, we are facing an issue that can and may well split the church, so which is more important? I suggest that we cancel all annual conferences so that this training can take place. Leave the administrative details to the annual conferences' staffs.

4)   At this time, the various annual conferences will have to come to grips with where they are on the subject of the noninclusion clause among the clergy. Regardless of the intense training, there will be a significant split among the clergy. Some will be in favor of removal of the noninclusion clause, and some will not. Others will be ambivalent and see it as an uncritical issue. The clergy will be given time to have discussions among themselves and the presenters from all three sessions. Then a vote will be taken. The vote will be to eliminate negative portions of the Doctrine that refer to homosexuals and homosexual practice. The following sections on marriage and ordination will be stripped : "¶ 304.3: The practice of homosexuality is incompatible with Christian teaching. Therefore self-avowed practicing homosexuals are not to be certified as candidates, ordained as ministers, or appointed to serve in The United Methodist Church." "¶ 341.6: Ceremonies that celebrate homosexual unions shall not be conducted by our ministers and shall not be conducted in our churches." Also, the financial statements in ¶ 613 and ¶ 806.9.

The intent is not to make statements regarding the acceptance of homosexual practice, unions, and ordination, but to eliminate the distinction between homosexual and heterosexual. In other words, to go back to pre-1972 days in the UMC. Of course, the clergy does not have the authority to make the changes in the Discipline, but it is a first step for eliminating the noninclusion clause. This is similar to the compromise made by Revs. Slaughter and Hamilton with one major difference: It says nothing (still keeping the nondiscrimination language in the social doctrine) about churches having gay weddings or ordination of gays. If this change in language does eventually pass, pastors will have the right to marry or not marry as they understand. Boards of Ordained

Ministry will recommend those they deem to have the proper gifts and graces for ministry. During this study being done by the elders of the church, it is important that the PR pot of the various organizations not be stirred. Both advocate organizations on both sides need to keep quiet without stirring up the laity. The intent is a careful study of the issue in holy conferencing.

5)   Each elder is to begin a similar study in his or her appointed charge. The annual conferences need to supply materials, including videos of the various presenters from the annual conferences and biblical teaching materials. Pastors can use Sunday School, Wednesday Bible study, and sermons to educate their congregants.

This task is not easy. It was not easy for Adam Hamilton who started the process in his church years ago. He first published an educational essay on homosexuality in 2001.[120] In 2008 he published the sermon on homosexuality that he preached in 2004.[121] He also told of the painful fallout from the sermon in the aftermath. Integrity is not an easy path. Pastors should make an effort to explain the issue as objectively as possible, Pastors who disagree with the direction the church is going should still be able to educate their congregations on the issue. The issue of homosexuality cannot be ignored. There will be a lot of wringing of hands and gnashing of teeth throughout the church. The alternative is schism.

6)   At each annual conference throughout the connection, a resolution should be brought up to eliminate the portions of the Discipline excluding homoeroticism.

If people are educated scientifically/medically, relationally, and biblically, these resolutions will pass in most of the annual conferences in the United States. Africa is unlikely; there is too much cultural bias. The likelihood of success will be mixed depending on the particular annual conference. The alternative of not providing

---

120   Hamilton, *Confronting the Controversies*, pp. 112-128.
121   Hamilton, *Seeing Gray*, pp. 165-187.

education and training is schism. Although there may not be a complete resolution, the issue will be discussed, and there will be clarity on where each annual conference stands.

7)   By the time of General Conference, the issue will be *fait accompli*; that is, we should be able to strip out the language added in 1972. Unfortunately, General Conference 2016 will be over by then, so actually stripping the exclusionary language from the Discipline cannot occur until 2020.

That does not mean we will all be in agreement. Some churches will not accept gay weddings or gay pastors, but some churches today do not accept cross-ethnic appointments or women pastors. Not all pastors will agree to do gay weddings. This is but a first step in reaching a common point of practice within the connectional, episcopal United Methodist Church. It is possible that we will come to the conclusion that the current Discipline is correct as it stands, but it has to stand against biblical scrutiny.

One of the things that has been the impetus behind the debate has been the biblical obedience of clergy willing to sacrifice their careers (but not callings) by officiating at same-sex weddings. To conservatives this violates the covenant expressed in the Discipline and allegiance expressed at ordination. Which allegiance is higher? I perceive these acts as similar to the various civil rights events of the 1960s and beyond. Civil rights demonstrations pushed us to do the right thing as a nation, although with great pain. The laws and practices were wrong. Today, those pastors who are performing gay marriages (unions, blessings, etc.) are pushing the United Methodist Church to do the right thing. Resolution will be painful, chaotic, and destructive in the short run. Thirty years from now, the church will look back and wonder why there was such a big fight that kept us from fulfilling our true mission: making disciples of Jesus Christ for the transformation of the world.

I pledge to officiate at same-sex weddings when and if asked.

BIBLIOGRAPHY

Alexander, J. Neil. *This Far by Grace: A Bishop's Journey Through Questions About Homosexuality*. Lanham, Maryland: Cowley Publications, 2003.

Alter, Robert. *The Five Books of Moses: A Translation with Commentary*. New York: W. W. Norton & Company, 2004.

Alter, Robert. *Genesis: Translation and Commentary*. New York: W. W. Norton & Company, 1996.

Boswell, John. *Same Sex Unions in Premodern Europe*. New York: Vintage Books, 1994.

Boswell, John. *Christianity, Social Tolerance, and Homosexuality: for People of Western Europe from the Beginning of the Christian Era to the Fourteenth Century*. Chicago: University of Chicago Press, 1980.

Brueggemann, Walter. *Genesis* (Interpretation: A Biblical Commentary for Teaching and Preaching). Atlanta : John Knox Press, 1982.

Cheng, Patrick S. *Radical Love: An Introduction to Queer Theology*. New York: Seabury Books, 2011.

Childs, James M., Jr. (ed.) *Faithful Conversations: Christian Perspectives on Homosexuality*. Minneapolis: Fortress Press, 2003.

Countryman, L. William. *Dirt, Greed, & Sex: Sexual Ethics in the New Testament and Their Implications for Today*, revised edition. Minneapolis: Fortress Press, 2007.

Countryman, L. William. *The New Testament Is in Greek: A Short Course for Exegetes*. Grand Rapids, Michigan: William B. Eerdmans Publishing Company, 1993.

Dwyer, John F. *Those 7 References: A Study of 7 References to Homosexuality in The Bible*. Self-published, 2000.

Fee, Gordon D. *The First Epistle to the Corinthians* (The New International Commentary on the New Testament). Grand Rapids, Michigan: William B. Eerdmans Publishing Company, 1987.

Fitzmyer, Joseph A. *Romans: A New Translation with Introduction and Commentary* (The Anchor Bible, vol. 33). New York: Doubleday, 1993.

Furnish, Victor Paul. *The Moral Teaching of Paul: Selected Issues*, 3rd edition. Nashville: Abingdon Press, 2009.

Freedman, David Noel (ed.) *The Anchor Bible Dictionary*. New York: Doubleday, 1992.

Fretheim, Terence E. *The Book of Genesis* (The New Interpreter's Bible, Volume I). Nashville: Abingdon Press, 1994.

Gagnon, Robert A. J. *The Bible and Homosexual Practice: Texts and Hermeneutics*. Nashville: Abingdon Press, 2001.

Hamilton, Adam. *When Christians Get It Wrong*. Nashville: Abingdon Press, 2013.

Hamilton, Adam. *Seeing Gray in a World of Black and White: Thoughts on Religion, Morality, and Politics*. Nashville: Abingdon Press, 2008.

Hamilton, Adam. *Making Sense of the Bible: Rediscovering the Power of Scripture Today*. New York: HarperOne, 2014.

Hamilton, Adam. *Confronting the Controversies: A Christian Look at the Tough Issues*. Nashville: Abingdon Press, 2001.

Helminiak, Daniel A. *What the Bible Really Says about Homosexuality*. New Mexico: Alamo Square Press, 2000.

Hays, Richard B. *First Corinthians* (Interpretation: A Bible Commentary for Teaching and Preaching). Louisville, John Knox Press, 1997.

Job, Rueben P. and Neil M. Alexander (eds). *Finding Our Way: Love and Law in the United Methodist Church*. Nashville: Abingdon Press, 2014.

Hultgren, Arland J. "Being Faithful to the Scriptures: Romans 1:26-27 as a Case in Point," *Word & World*, Vol. 14, No. 3, Summer 1994, pp. 315-325.

Kaiser, Walter C. *The Book of Leviticus* (The New Interpreter's Bible, Volume I). Nashville: Abingdon Press, 1994.

Kalin, Everett R. *Currents in Theology and Mission*, Vol. 30, No. 6, December 2003, pp. 423-432.

Keener, Craig S. *1-2 Corinthians* (The New Cambridge Bible Commentary). Cambridge: Cambridge University Press, 2005.

Kuhn, Karl A. *Currents in Theology and Mission*, Vol. 33, No. 4, August 2006, pp. 313-329.

Lings, K. Renato. *Love Lost in Translation: Homosexuality and the Bible*. Trafford Publishing, www.trafford.com, 2013.

Martin, Dale B. *Arsenokoites and Malakos: Meanings and Consequences*. http://www.clgs.org/arsenokoit%C3%A9s-and-malakos-meanings-and-consequences.

Miller, James E. "The Practices of Romans 1:26: Homosexual OR Heterosexual?" *Novum Testamentum*, Vol. 37, No. 1, January 1995, pp. 1-11.

Niebuhr, H. Richard. *Christ and Culture*. New York: Harper & Row, Publishers, 1951.

Olson, Dennis T. *The Book of Judges.*(The New Interpreter's Bible, Volume 2). Nashville: Abingdon Press, 1998.

Rogers, Jack. *Jesus, the Bible and Homosexuality: Explode the Myths, Heal the Church*. Westminster: John Knox Press, 2009.

Sampley, J. Paul. *The First Letter to the Corinthians* (The New Interpreter's Bible, Volume 10). Nashville: Abingdon Press, 2002.

Sider, Ronald J. *Just Generosity*, 2nd ed. Grand Rapids, Michigan: Baker Books, 2007.

Smith, Mark D. "Ancient Bisexuality and the Interpretation of Romans 1:26-27," *Journal of the American Academy of Religion*, Vol. 64, No. 2, Summer 1996, pp. 223-256.

"Council of Bishops requests complaint against Talbert," http://
    umcconnections.org/2013/11/15/council-bishops-re-
    quest-complaint-talbert/.

Via, Dan O. and Robert A. J. Gagnon. *Homosexuality and the Bible:
    Two Views*. Minneapolis: Fortress Press, 2003

Vines, Matthew. *God and the Gay Christian: The Biblical Case in
    Support of Same-Sex Relationships*. Convergent Books; Reprint
    edition (June 16, 2015).

Wallis, Jim. *Rediscovering Values: A Guide for Economic and Moral
    Recovery*. New York: Howard Books, 2011.

Wright, N. T. *The Letter to the Romans* (The New Interpreter's Bible,
    Volume 10). Nashville: Abingdon Press, 2002.

STEVE KINDLE

I'M RIGHT
AND
YOU'RE WRONG

WHY WE DISAGREE ABOUT THE BIBLE
AND
WHAT TO DO ABOUT IT

Topical
Line
Drives

Volume 16

Why do well-meaning,
intelligent people disagree about
the Bible?

This text is profound without
being preachy, and inspires the reader
to claim a faith that is adventurous
and world-changing. One of the
best presentations of the progressive
Christian vision I have read.

Bruce Epperly, PhD
Author of *Process Theology:
Embracing Adventure with God* and
*A Center in the Cyclone:
Twenty-first Century Clergy Self-care*

Reframing
a
Relevant Faith

C. Drew Smith

MORE FROM ENERGION PUBLICATIONS

Personal Study

Holy Smoke! Unholy Fire	Bob McKibben	$14.99
The Jesus Paradigm	David Alan Black	$17.99
When People Speak for God	Henry Neufeld	$17.99
The Sacred Journey	Chris Surber	$11.99

Christian Living

It's All Greek to Me	David Alan Black	$3.99
Grief: Finding the Candle of Light	Jody Neufeld	$8.99
My Life Story	Becky Lynn Black	$14.99
Crossing the Street	Robert LaRochelle	$16.99
Life as Pilgrimage	David Moffett-Moore	14.99

Bible Study

Learning and Living Scripture	Lentz/Neufeld	$12.99
From Inspiration to Understanding	Edward W. H. Vick	$24.99
Philippians: A Participatory Study Guide	Bruce Epperly	$9.99
Ephesians: A Participatory Study Guide	Robert D. Cornwall	$9.99
Ecclesiastes: A Participatory Study Guide	Russell Meek	$9.99

Theology

Creation in Scripture	Herold Weiss	$12.99
Creation: the Christian Doctrine	Edward W. H. Vick	$12.99
The Politics of Witness	Allan R. Bevere	$9.99
Ultimate Allegiance	Robert D. Cornwall	$9.99
History and Christian Faith	Edward W. H. Vick	$9.99
The Journey to the Undiscovered Country	William Powell Tuck	$9.99
Process Theology	Bruce G. Epperly	$4.99

Ministry

Clergy Table Talk	Kent Ira Groff	$9.99
Out of This World	Darren McClellan	$24.99

Generous Quantity Discounts Available
Dealer Inquiries Welcome
Energion Publications — P.O. Box 841
Gonzalez, FL 32560
Website: http://energionpubs.com
Phone: (850) 525-3916

www.ingramcontent.com/pod-product-compliance
Lightning Source LLC
LaVergne TN
LVHW011203080426
835508LV00007B/576